Praise for

SHINE

Stories to Inspire You to

DREAM BIG, FEAR LESS & BLAZE YOUR OWN TRAIL

"*SHINE!* spotlights amazing and inspiring female leaders and entrepreneurs with candid stories to share. It demonstrates what happens when we move beyond our fears and what we 'ought to do' as prescribed by others and truly acknowledge our gifts and true essence. When that happens, as these women so beautifully describe, they became stronger and more empowered. You can too. Read and be amazed by them and by the possibilities inherent in you."

- **DR. JO ANNE WHITE**, Certified Life, Leadership and Business Coach, producer, radio host, best-selling author, and Energy Master Teacher

"When you live under a cloud from past experiences, it dims the beauty that is available to you every day. To become your beautiful self, and truly shine the way you are meant to, means letting go and leaving behind what no longer supports you. It is through the loss that you see a new path to expand and through the pain that you become free. Free to live in the light of your authentic self. These powerful women who share their stories in *SHINE!* exemplify the courage it takes to truly transform."

- **MAL DUANE**, Midlife Transformation Coach

"Our happy future is always before us. All we need to do is choose it. The inspirational stories in *SHINE!* will inspire you to keep going, no matter how dark the road looks, because on the other side of where you are is a world of joy, possibility, and happiness."

- **EVELINE JURRY**, creator of the Positive Separation Method, author of Happy Again! The Art of Positive Separation

"The quality of brightness reflected in these stories is sure to dazzle and delight you! What makes *SHINE!* a must-read is an authentic intensity; each author inspires by sharing how to blaze a trail through some darkness. Together, a timeless constellation shimmers on the pages to show you the way."

- **LORE RAYMOND**, best-selling author, Writing and Creativity Catalyst

"The amazing stories within *SHINE!* are powerful narratives of bravery and courage. Each author shows us how they were able to overcome obstacles and step forward to live passionately and fearlessly. By telling these stories, these stellar women inspire us to dream and step forward to do so for ourselves."

- **LAURA CLARK**, Soul Coaching® Master Practitioner & Trainer

"Women everywhere are cheering for *SHINE!* Stories to Inspire You To Dream Big, Fear Less and Blaze Your Own Trail. Within these pages, you will find twenty four stories to inspire your own metamorphosis. If you are looking to step out from the shadows of your life, look no further."

- **LISA HUTCHISON, LMHC,** licensed psychotherapist & writing coach

"*SHINE!* will take you on a journey of transformation, as you will see a piece of yourself in most every chapter of the book. These women have dug deep to allow us to see their innermost fears even while expanding their own shining souls. Get ready to dream big and shine!"

- **LARA JAYE,** Intuitive Executive Coach

"An empowering collective of stories of courage and transformation! If you are a woman who has faced challenges that threatened to keep you hidden or playing small, *SHINE!* is a must read. As you read through the powerful and life-changing experiences of these women, they will inspire you to overcome your own challenges, encourage you to stop hiding and to finally be brave enough to step into the brilliance of who you are and share the sacred gifts you were born to share!"

- **KIM TURCOTTE,** Women's Empowerment Expert and founder of The Goddess School

"In my opinion, *SHINE!* is a must-read for ALL women. *SHINE!* offers a view of lives impacted by obstacles, ultimately leading them to be liberated from their fears to living their true life's purpose. The poignant stories of these incredible women will move and enchant you. Beyond inspiring!"

- **DONA RUTOWICZ, LCSW,** Expert Relationship Coach

"I love traveling through the pages and words of the wonderful stories shared by the women who wrote *SHINE!* I find myself in their experiences. I have faced the same fears. I have been in the prison of limited beliefs. I have lived a small and compromised life, too. No more! As I step into my life, on my terms, their stories make me laugh, cry, cheer, feel proud and get more courageous to live this magnificent life fully. I will come back to these stories over and over for continued inspiration."

- **RACHEL KIEFFER,** Holistic Health Coach and Women Health Circles Coach

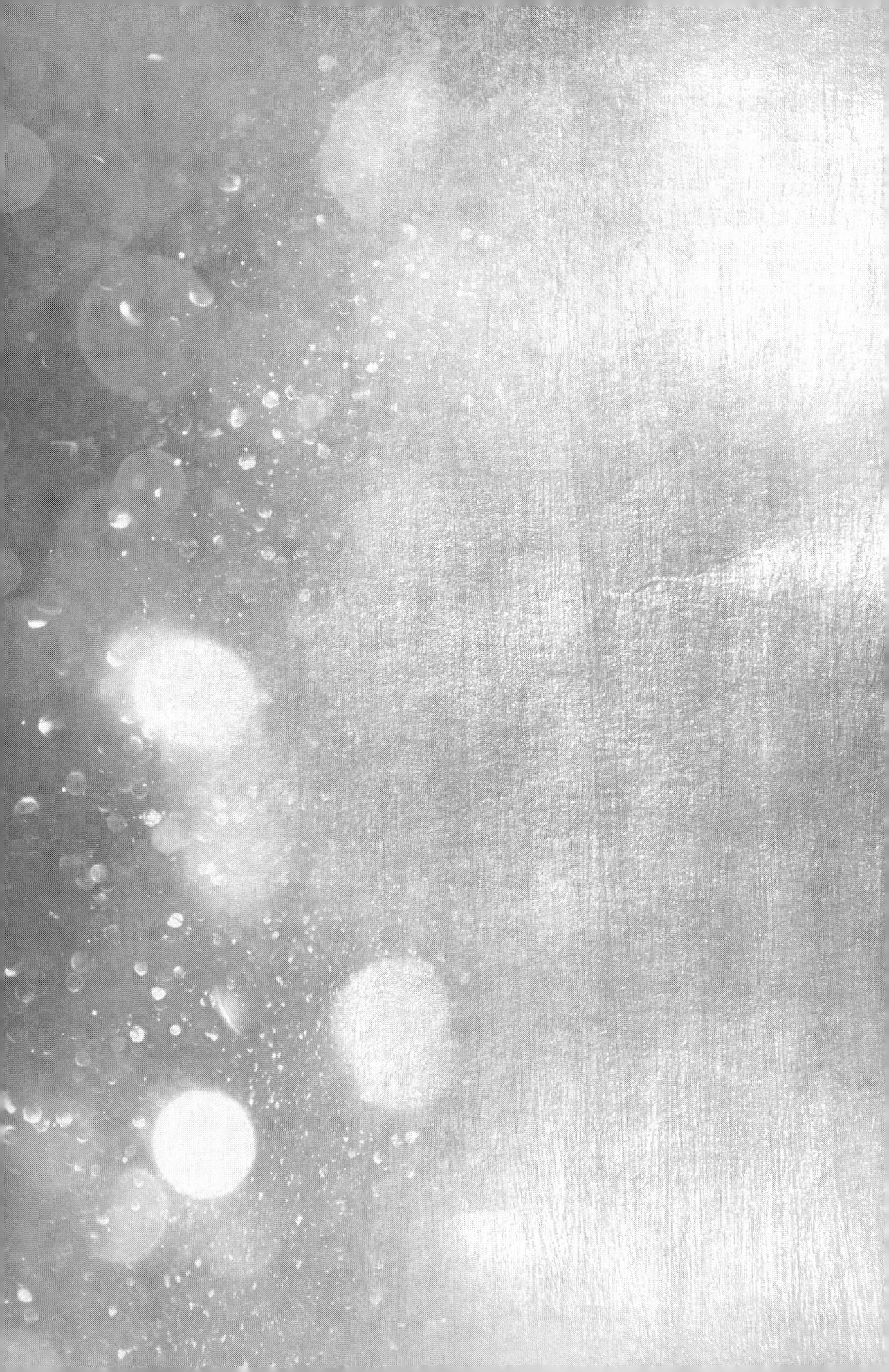

FOREWORD

Kristine Carlson

This question begs an answer from each of us. You may even feel it nag at you as your soul calls you to do *something* to be remembered by. Yet, so many of us focus on those times in our lives where we had fallen into the shadows—a spiraling marriage, a frustrating career, a role of some kind that sucked the passion right out of us and dulled our light like a waning moon. But, even on the dark days, we must remember that this pursuit of purpose is a natural part of the life journey, and in fact, it's a mission we signed up for the day we were born. It's an awakening to and a remembering of why we came to this earth. Consider this your beautiful charge, your most human duty: to answer with fullness and authenticity, *"What is that special thing I am here to do?"*

When we realize, from time to time, that we are living a life that doesn't fit us (and we will *all* encounter these poignant moments), change is inevitable. Yet, that essential pivot often feels too far and too big, perhaps on the other side of an insurmountable wall of fear. But the pain of holding onto the "known" will eventually be enough to embolden us to shatter the barrier and step forward into our destiny. And, remember this: we get to choose how we move forward. At the fork in the road, you may turn left to walk deeper into the dark forest and into the shadows. Or, you may turn right and climb the mountain to the summit where you finally reach the top of a vast vista. It's a hard journey upward, perhaps, but it culminates in the spacious freedom where you can spread your arms and fling open your heart. Only from there can you feel the power of the myriad possibilities that await you.

The poignant stories in *SHINE!* show us that transformation *is* possible as each woman shares her personal journey of breaking free to be herself. Listening to the voices that resonate deep within our own hearts is the first true step any one of us can take as we search for the meaning of our lives. We have to remember who we are to remember why we came. Within the pages of this book, each woman's story demonstrates the courage required to lean into fear and the beautiful vibrancy that emerges when we do so. You'll see that these brave souls broke down the barriers that had held them captive and finally answered the call of their souls to show up in the fullest expression of their true nature.

The Greek definition of happiness states that we experience the most joy when we are pursuing a life that fulfills our human potential. And conversely, it would also be true that we experience deep sadness and malaise when we are off course and in the fog of a life that no longer fits us (or perhaps never did). It's easy to overlook purpose if we choose to simply survive—but when we decide that survival isn't enough, then we take steps to thrive. And in thriving, we reclaim aspects of ourselves that we've left behind. By allowing the whispers of our souls and the pulls of our passion to lead the way forward we can all grow to express from our truest nature all that we are, bringing us to the gateway of bliss.

The stories shared in *SHINE!* show courage and whisper hope, and they also show that the price we pay for staying in the shadows is too great. Ignoring the call of our hearts inhibits our true expression. Your soul came here to shine; do not settle for less than your heart's true desire.

We did not enter this life adventure just to play small and be invisible. There's something unique for each of us to do, to be, and to share in our brief and precious human experience. Much of your journey, my friend, will be breaking down the barriers that stand in the way. It takes courage and strength, but you're made for this—made to let your remarkable soul shine unapologetically as you dare to live as big as your universe allows.

Thank you to the women in this book for sharing their journeys with us. Shine on with all that you are, and all that you can be. The world is waiting for you to unleash your light so others can see.

Kristine Carlson
New York Times best-selling author, world-renowned
speaker and retreat leader

Table of
CONTENTS

Chapter Three | GO YOUR OWN WAY

Chapter Four | TRUST YOUR INNER KNOWING

Chapter Five | CLAIM THE SPOTLIGHT

SHINE!

Stories to Inspire You to

DREAM BIG, FEAR LESS & BLAZE YOUR OWN TRAIL

INTRODUCTION

Linda Joy, Publisher

Do you remember the dreams you had as a child? Those moments when you would fearlessly express that you were going to be a doctor, a dancer, a writer, or a teacher? Your dreams were big and expansive, and you could feel them in the depths of your being. In those moments of dreaming, you were connected to your true essence—your authentic self, the sacred place where your light shines brightest.

So many of us, at one time or another, have dimmed our light and hidden our authentic selves. Maybe we felt we had to wear a mask, or live by the "shoulds" and "have-tos" of our family or society. Maybe we were told we were "too much" or "too loud," and so we made ourselves smaller to fit in. Maybe we didn't want to rock the boat in a relationship, or got too comfortable letting others set the parameters in our lives.

The reasons were different, but the results were the same. Somewhere between childhood and adulthood, between innocence and experience, we made ourselves smaller, made our light dimmer, and smothered the essence of our authentic selves.

Imagine, a beautiful glowing light—a gem—within your heart that is covered in layers of muck. Those layers are covering up the brilliance you came here to be—the truth of who you are. They are your fears, your false beliefs, your expectations, and your everyday busyness. They are what keeps you playing small, making excuses, and choosing your "shoulds" over your joy.

It's time to wash them clean.

I've come to believe that we are all here to live authentically, share our unique gifts, and shine our light to illuminate the path for others. The only way to reclaim our light is to go deep into the truth of ourselves so we can excavate the gem.

On my own healing journey, which began twenty-eight years ago, I set out to uncover the layers of shame, self-doubt, insecurity, and false beliefs that were muddying my connection to my light. Over time, I came to know my true essence and sense what was possible for me—and for all the amazing women in my world who were in hiding, just like I had been.

Then, one day, about ten years ago, everything came to a standstill. I had a huge "A-ha!" moment. I realized that things in my world had shifted. I had changed. I had healed. And now, I was at a moment of choice. Would I keep playing small and catering to my fears to avoid rocking the boat of my life … or would I clear the final layers of muck from my authentic self, stand up, stand out, and shine with everything I had?

I chose to shine. And I have never looked back.

Today, as a best-selling publisher, Visibility Catalyst, Authentic Marketing Mentor, and intuitive, I support heart-centered female entrepreneurs in breaking through the blocks that keep them separated from their own Sacred Visibility™, while providing a global media platform across which they can share their message, shine their lights, and transform lives.

Every time a woman steps into her divine brilliance and courageously chooses to shine instead of shrink, a ripple of transformation is sent out into the world. That ripple becomes a wave that others can ride. One moment of truth can start a movement. I've seen it happen over and over again.

All of the stories in this book are from women who have chosen to shine in their lives—to be their own North Stars, to be their own guiding lights. They share the moments when they decided to take off their masks and stop playing small in their lives, relationships, missions, health, and work. These moments—whether big or small, momentous or quiet—triggered a landslide of change that brought down the walls behind which these women had been hiding. Freed and empowered, they then stepped onto life's stage like the superstars they are.

When they chose to share their intimate stories of personal growth, realization, and transformation, they did so knowing that it would support, inspire, and empower *you*. It's time for you to shine your light, dream big, and blaze your trail in this world. Let these stories be hands for you to hold as you step onto your own stage.

My beautiful friend, the world needs you now more than ever. Read these stories, laugh, cry, and journal using the reflection questions. Wash clean the layers of pain and shame that are keeping your light covered up. Then come join us as we set the world ablaze!

Shine, baby, shine!

With brilliant love,
Linda Joy

Chapter One

OWN YOUR GIFTS

THE POWER OF PERMISSION

Jami Hearn

"Do what lights you up!"

Seems like sound advice, if you know what that "what" might be! For a long time, I wasn't so fortunate. I lived in the delusion that money and material things would create that feeling of being lit up—but I couldn't have been farther from the truth.

I was eight months pregnant with a huge baby, and could barely waddle myself around the room of musty old record books where I spent the summer sweating. As an associate in a law firm that was the textbook definition of a "patriarchal institution," I wasn't granted any clemency. There were no set hours, and the firm paid for my cell phone so there were no justifiable excuses for not answering. However, jobs were not easy to come by, and I'd just spent a bundle on a law degree, so even though my work was both anxiety-provoking and soul-crushing, I trudged on.

Every morning, I had to talk myself off the ledge. My career had barely begun, and already I was burning myself out. I reminded myself that this was the stepping stone to creating the life I had always dreamed of—a life of wealth, happiness, and freedom. If I could just get the day started, I told myself, the end of the day would arrive quickly, and then (hopefully) I could rest.

The day of my first performance review was an especially raw and power-stripping one. I walked into that review knowing that I had busted my ass for the firm. I worked fourteen-hour days, and drove more than 500 miles per week. I always showed up to meet clients with a smile, ready to put them at ease around whatever drama or disaster was brewing. Meanwhile, the jerks in Armani suits reaped all the financial rewards.

When the managing partner entered the conference room, he chose the furthest chair from where I sat. His words hissed from between his thin, snake-like lips.

"Your performance has been subpar. You seem to be very distracted by things less important than your job. You aren't dedicated enough, and you haven't brought in enough new clients."

As the words rolled off his forked tongue, I recoiled in shock. "When you hired me, you told me to make sure the clients assigned to me were taken care of. You said that you were the rainmaker, and that it wasn't my responsibility to acquire new clients for the firm." Even as I spoke, I knew my response was a waste of energy. This was how the partners justified refusing raises or promotions to female attorneys in the firm.

"You are lucky to be keeping your job," the partner retorted. "We expect that you will demonstrate a higher degree of dedication to your career and our clients from now on. And, little girl, your insubordinate responses will not be tolerated. Don't waste any more time here. You have your worth to prove—if you desire to stay employed."

I knew I was good at what I was doing, and that the managing partner was dead wrong about me. But in that moment, the truth about the expectations being placed on me came clearly into focus. I was never going to be "good enough." How could I be, when I had other things (like the baby in my womb) that consumed my attention? As a mother, I was never going to make partner in this firm.

Thank the Goddess that my vision, and my belief in myself, allowed me to see my next right step—and it was *not* back into the courthouse.

On Sunday, four days after my disastrous review, I was sitting on the deck in my backyard when I was overcome by a physical vibration. It was like a waterfall of golden light was washing over me—showing me that this is who I am, and that I do not have to tolerate anything less than happiness, joy, and prosperity.

I was done making a living by defeating opponents. No longer would someone have to lose in order for me to survive.

The next day, Monday, I resigned from that law firm. The managing partner wouldn't meet with me, nor would he take a phone call from me. So, I left him a voicemail message and a letter of resignation, and set off to find who I really was and where I really wanted to travel.

When I threw open the front door of that dreary, dank office, I noticed the birds chirping and the sweet smell of magnolia flowers in the air. Had those been here the whole time? I wondered. Or had the shedding of obligation and misalignment lifted me into greater awareness?

The next version of me did not just magically appear. Rather, connecting with my authentic self has been a process of evolution. Each layer peeled away has allowed me to gain more clarity around what truly lights me up.

Once I was no longer bogged down by my soul-sucking job, I started working with my spiritual support team more closely. My tribe consisted of mentors in my daily life, and my guides and teachers in the spirit realms. I invested time and money into myself—after all, if I didn't care enough about me to take these steps for myself, who would? I went to classes. I opened to receive messages and anything else the universe had to offer me. Most importantly, I allowed myself to get to know, and love, my true self.

There were days I didn't know who the hell I was, or what the hell I was doing, but even in those dark moments of questioning, I trusted my intuition and believed in myself. I was in there, even if I couldn't see me. Every day, I came more into focus. I became a little more comfortable with who I was becoming. The me who was emerging had always been just below the surface; I just had to remember who she was.

My calling—to be of service to spiritual women—turns out to be exactly what lights me up. I have the unbelievable privilege of being able to offer healing and guidance to women on the path of spiritual growth, leaving them better for having known me. Now, when my work keeps me up at night, it's because of my giddy excitement as I feel the healing that both my clients and I enjoy from my work.

Recently, I did a gallery reading where I shared messages for the people in the audience; one in particular was especially meaningful. It was for a woman, Claire, who was self-employed and struggling. I could see myself in her story—but it was her grandmother who shared through me.

"My dear, you chose this path for a reason, but as you acquire new knowledge and experience, you are free to make any choice that serves you, at any time."

Claire was not so convinced that she could change her mind, "But I've built my identity around this business," she said. "I don't know where it stops and I start. I don't want people to judge me and think that I failed. What if they think I'm not good enough?"

Grandmother redirected Claire's focus. "You are not bound to continue on the path of struggle. You, yourself, hold the responsibility to honor who you are at a soul level. Let go of the emotional attachment to what anyone else thinks. You are empowered to step fully into who you genuinely want to be."

As the message was heard, I witnessed Claire receiving the gift of permission and alignment, and I felt privileged to be a catalyst for her to take her first step forward.

Permission is powerful. All we need is *permission* to be exactly who we are; when we give that to ourselves, we step out of the broom closet and into our greatness. I gave myself that permission; now, I empower other amazing women to allow themselves that same authority.

To assist in keeping myself grounded in this truth, (because it is so easy to become distracted), I created a sacred space in my home where I can retreat whenever I need to ground in my own power. In this space, I can be with myself and exclude the influence of variables that are not in alignment with me. Of course, I have to reemerge at some point—but after I renew my belief in my authenticity, those external forces (to be defined as nay-saying friends or family, or the negativity that flows from society) are stripped of power over me.

These days, I get excited for Monday mornings, and for the new opportunities and souls I encounter every week. I hear the birds chirping and smell the flowers, every day. My morning ritual is one of ease and grace. I have my coffee on the porch and connect with nature. (Or, sometimes, nature connects with me, like the day a bird pooped on me.) I have awareness of the reciprocity of the universe, and of the vibration with which I surround myself. I have the luxury of creating my day on my terms, and in the vibration absolutely aligned with my divine soul. I thrive on working with amazing clients who exist in such a high vibration. I live in service, and take action to benefit both myself and those whose paths I cross. My purpose is in alignment with creating healing and awareness for my clients, and it's my privilege to illuminate the path for others to walk.

And I would never have known any of this if I hadn't given myself permission to walk out of my old life and be lit up in a new one.

Reflection

Is there a place in your life where you feel you will never be "good enough"? If so, what steps can you take to change that situation so you can shine in your true greatness?

Do you feel that someone else has to "lose" in order for you to "win" or prosper? How can you shift to a scenario where everyone is uplifted?

Where are you tethering yourself to a path of struggle? What new choice can you make, right now, to be in greater ease and alignment?

THE STORY OF A LIFETIME

Dr. Catherine Hayes, CPCC

I've thought about writing a book for most of my adult life. Many people encouraged me along the way to write my story, and a book felt like the most natural format to share it. It was my dream to publish my story, to share—and in doing so, perhaps put to rest—the hardships of my childhood.

Somehow, though, the book didn't come to life. I got so busy with my life and my career that my dream of being an author kept getting pushed to the back burner, where it sat for years … actually, for decades.

Then, when I was in my mid-forties, I had a life-changing accident. I don't have any memory of the accident itself, but it was (quite literally) a whack on the head. I used to joke that I would need to get whacked on the head to "wake up" in my life. But when it actually happened, I didn't know what to do with it at first.

At the time, I was well-established in an academic career and on the tenure track at Harvard University. I had been in school, in one way or another, for my whole life: first, as a full-time student until the age of thirty-three, earning a Master's and two doctoral degrees; and later as a faculty member. School had been my safe place since

I was a child; there, I shone, and was recognized for my hard work and achievements.

But my accident changed things for me. It forced me to slow down, and look at what I was really creating in my life. I began a deep inner journal of introspection, looking at my life and how I was showing up in it, from various angles, some of which I had never considered before. I began to see how busy I had made myself, and how far I had traveled from my heart's desires to create a life lived in response to the outside world. My book was just one of many dreams that I'd shelved over the years as I pursued success and academic achievement.

Suddenly, my life had taken a right turn. Inside, I knew I was heading away from the traditional life of an academician. I didn't know what was to come, but I could no longer maintain my status quo. Things were changing fast, and it was becoming more and more painful to deny who I was in favor of what I wanted others to think of me.

A year to the day after my accident, I attended a workshop on the Enneagram led by Russ Hudson and Gayle Scott. It revealed aspects of my personality that rocked me to my core, but also gave me a new, more holistic perspective around the choices I'd made and the paths I'd chosen in my life. As a Type Three, I was driven to succeed because I wanted to prove something about myself to others—namely, that I was worthy of love and recognition.

When I returned from that workshop, I sat at my desk at Harvard and, for the first time, felt out of place there. I knew that I could no longer live the life I had created up to this point. I could no longer stay in my safe place—but I didn't know where else to go.

What followed that realization was an intense spiritual journey of discovery, forgiveness, and letting go. I had to peel away so many layers of habitual thought and protective behavior that, when I was done, I felt naked. Bare.

It was then that I knew it was time to start writing my book.

Funny that the book didn't come to life because of my story, but rather because I had finally unraveled my story and moved beyond it. I had found a place of freedom and forgiveness, and from that place I was able to see the true value of my experiences to myself, and to others. Writing was no longer just about overcoming the challenges of my childhood, but about using my story to uplift others and witness them in their own process of discovery.

Writing my story was challenging. It brought me back into the pain of my childhood in a new way—but also allowed me to see the great value in each lesson I learned, and find closure around those pieces of my past that were still unresolved. When I started to get caught up in the task of simply stating my story, my editor helped me expand my perspective through insightful questions.

Then, as I was starting to dive deeply into the book, life got in the way. Somehow, it seems that just as we decide to go "all in," we get derailed by life events. It's as if the Universe is trying to test our dedication. As I began to put pen to paper in earnest, I was sidetracked by a house fire, the long-term hospitalization of a loved one, and multiple family crises. Combined, these factors took two years away from my writing—but I came back stronger than ever, and in complete alignment with divine timing.

It turns out that writing a book isn't just about putting words on paper—at least, not when you're writing the kind of book that I did. Instead, it's about processing the story of a lifetime, with all of its attachments and triggers, and transforming that story into something that will inspire and teach others. Although I wouldn't have guessed it when I started, writing was very much a part of my journey toward wholeness and healing. In the process, I looked deeply into my old wounds, and saw them differently; they were, in a way, the cracks through which my light could now truly shine. My moments of pain become others' lessons as well as my own. The creation of this book was an unfolding of my soul.

When I chose to share my story with the world, I chose to allow myself to express myself in the world in a more robust and expansive way. I believe that as each of us shares our individual story—our individual expression of being—we will begin to see how connected and similar we all are. As each of us contributes to the fabric of human experience, we weave the truth of our reality.

Writing my book was the final step in a full-circle journey from my early life of strife, pain, and struggle to a life of peace, contentment, and fulfillment. No longer am I protected by the walls of academia; I'm out there in the world for all to see and judge. It's a vulnerable place to be. Recently, I explained to a friend that it reminds me of the dreams I used to have about teaching a class in my nightgown. The vulnerability and exposure is palpable and frightening—and yet, at the same time, I know that this needed to come forth from me. This knowing is stronger than my fear, stronger than my doubt.

With my book in hand, I'm shining in the new world I've created for myself. I'm also standing side by side with so many other women who have owned their voices and claimed their space in the world—and with all the others who, like me, are just stepping forward. No matter where we are in our journey, we can look to one another with compassion and respect, seeing the commonality of our experiences and the richness of our weaving. Our lights shine brightly, and in unison. Together, we illuminate the world.

Reflection

Is there a passion project you've been putting off? What is it and why haven't you started it yet?

Where are you using busyness as a shield or an excuse in your life? How can you give yourself space to breathe and expand?

Catherine found freedom from her story through sharing it. When, where, and with whom can you share your story in order to lift its weight?

SECRETS REVEALED

Cindy Hively

The most powerful "Yes!" I ever said to myself was when I chose to show up in my life as a modern-day Goddess, an embodiment of the Divine Feminine. Each day since that choice has been a process of surrendering to this wondrous gift in ways both authentic and magical. The last two years, in particular, have been an initiation into Priestess wisdom; as I cultivate deeper understanding and compassion for myself, I illuminate the ancient and mystical spiritual teachings for other women so that they, too, can heal and transform their lives.

My life hasn't always been this magical. Oh, Goddess, the darkness, the pure bleeding wounds that ran red and raw! These were secrets I held within.

And so my truth-telling begins.

My brother and I were raised in a good home. I will never doubt that my parents' love was anything but unconditional. We ate meals together as a family, and shared in conversations that left me full of giggles. We went to church on Sundays, and religion was a huge part of our lives. I was a true-believer, a Bible-thumping Baptist, and a "Daddy's girl" through and through. (My dad, a retired Marine, scared the bejesus out of my dates, so I rarely went out with the same guy twice!)

When I went to college, I showed up as a free spirit, always on the lookout for the next fun adventure. "Girls Just Wanna Have Fun" was my theme song. I didn't worry, or live in fear; I simply did what felt fun and exciting.

Things started to change after college, when I married my sweetheart a year after graduation. I loved him enough to say "I do," and I loved my baby girl, who was born just over a year later, even more. But the marriage didn't work. My husband was an alcoholic, and became abusive. After I left, he decided that ending his life with a bullet was the best path for him.

My second husband was a narcissist who cheated, lied, and abused without shame or conscience. He left in the middle of the night one night and never came back.

I shared very little about my "scarlet red" experiences, but I knew I was a topic of gossip at church. In my faith community, divorce wasn't an option. If you couldn't work it out, you zipped your lips and bore it like a "good girl." My so-called sins always took up space in the room, but it wasn't proper to air my dirty laundry, so hardly anyone knew my side of the story.

My family, friends, and peers never really knew who I was, or what I had endured. After years of keeping all of the shame and guilt inside, I barely recognized myself. I felt numb. I wasn't living authentically, or in alignment with my soul purpose and Divine intention. It took a serious health crisis and eight months in bed to wake me up to what I needed to shift in my life.

I'll never forget the first time I saw the word "Goddess." I had an awakening that was immediate. I could feel the word pulsating through my whole body. As I started researching, reading, and studying, I knew that I was finally beginning my Shero's journey. I would learn to stand in my power and own my truth, no matter what anyone else thought about it.

But how the heck could I even begin such a task? I was in deep fear. The only thing I could do was to surrender to the Divine.

By this time in my life, I was guarded. I hadn't gone to church in years. I found my spiritual connection in other places and spaces, but I rarely shared about it with others, especially my family. It was time to stop hiding, and release myself from the shame and judgment that was still hanging over my head. Being stuck in this energy was causing me to stagnate in both my physical body and my spiritual practice. Divine feminine is all about flow, but I was hanging on for dear life.

A conversation on meditation broke the ice with my parents. I was able to share my knowledge gently, from the perspective that the Bible teaches us to be meditative. Little by little, I shared more. There was a lot of fear there for me; I felt the pain of not living up to everyone else's standards. I desperately wanted my parents to be proud of who I had become, even though I had traveled way beyond being Daddy's Little Girl.

One day, while on the phone with my mom, I made reference to something in my past relationships. "Honey, I don't know how you've gotten through all of this," my mom shared.

I decided to be fully honest. "I lived my life in a fantasy to protect myself. I pretended everything was okay, and I even believed it. But I'm tired of the façade. I don't want to do it anymore."

Once again, my mom came through with affirmations of unconditional love. She said, "We will always love you, no matter what you think you have done, or will do."

Hearing those words created a monumental shift for me. As the teary mist settled, I received so much clarity. My intuition had told me to share with my mom in that moment, and I had received exactly what I needed.

I call my intuition my "light compass." We are each born with an intuitive nature; it is our inner guidance system. My intuitive responses have often taken me out of my comfort zone, but each time I honor them, I see that the leap was part of the Divine plan for me to show up authentically and share from my heart. Listening to my inner wisdom is a sacred act.

Many of us who are called to awaken the Divine within us through spiritual practice hold emotional residue, abuse, and trauma in our bodies. The more I reconnect with my physical, emotional, and spiritual self, the more I heal. Being in touch with myself, and healing the damaging thoughts that kept me locked in shame, was crucial to stepping into Priestesshood.

When I reached the place in my life where I felt called to share my stories with the world, it was incredibly scary. But as I opened up to other women, the more I saw that each story was a chance to create more healing—for them, and for me. It was like realizing that I had the cure for the common cold, but I'd been keeping it to myself all this time. The world *needs* me to show up fully.

I have allowed myself to answer my divine calling to play in nature, create herbal medicines, embody the Earth cycles and lunar rhythms, engage in rituals, and live in harmony with everyone around me. My relationships with my family and friends are amazing. Although much of what I practice is not part of their belief system, they respect my work and acknowledge its healing power. The part of sharing my story that I feared most—revealing my spiritual truths to my conservative friends and family, who might turn their backs on me or cast me out—ended up being one of the most healing parts of my growth process. The things I feared never materialized, and I learned that I could trust that inner voice that called me to share. More, when I stopped hiding my emotions, I found new ways to connect to others.

Today, I no longer feel ashamed of my past, and I've stopped judging myself for my experiences and choices. My spiritual journey is lived with daily intention and reverence. When I stand in my truth, I feel freedom. I certainly don't have to be perfect anymore; I just have to be me. And when I hold that space, everything I need to shine brightly in the world is there for me.

Reflection

Where are you holding onto shame or judgment in your life?

Is there something about your life, spiritual practice, or belief system that you're hiding from others? What are you afraid will happen if you speak your truth?

What miracles have happened when you've shared your truth? How can you hold those sacred experiences close to your heart so that you can continue to be truthful when it counts?

A GIFT OF LISTENING

Deborah Kevin

When I look back, I can't believe I didn't see the signs. They were all there, bright as a lighthouse beacon on a foggy night, flashing: *Warning, warning, warning*. There was the walking without crawling. Preoccupation with spinning wheels. Hyper-focus.

But I didn't see—until I sat under the hissing fluorescent lights in a psychiatrist's office coloring in circles on an intake form. There were so many black marks on my paper that it resembled reverse Swiss cheese. Even before Dr. H made his pronouncement, I knew. My son was on the autism spectrum.

"Jack's anxiety is so high that I recommend you put him on a low dose of Prozac," the doctor said. "It's been proven effective in young children." He went on to rattle off potential side effects in obligatory fashion, adding, "Less than two percent of children have any adverse reactions."

Two nights later my nine-year-old son told me I needed to hide the knives. "A monster is whispering in my ear, telling me to cut myself," Jack screamed. "Make it stop. Make it stop!"

Questions swirled inside my head. My thoughts seemed unable to latch onto anything reasonable.

I sat on the family room floor with my son held tight against my torso, my legs wrapped around his, and his arms crisscrossed against my chest. Tears streamed down my face while he screamed and thrashed. Was I doing the right thing keeping him like this? It felt as though I had imprisoned him.

A counselor friend of mine had shared this swaddling technique, which she used when the traumatized children with whom she worked got physically violent. "It'll keep him from hurting himself or others," she'd said.

So Jack lashed. I cried and knew in my gut that we'd made a mistake by putting him on Prozac.

My husband hovered over me, shifting his weight from foot to foot. The floorboards groaned with each movement, his anxiety ratcheting up my own. "Jack. Stop. It. This. Instant," he said, grinding each word out through clenched teeth.

Our recent marriage hadn't gotten off to a good start, and my new husband frequently complained that I let my youngest son off too easy. We argued daily behind closed doors.

"Please stop. You're making this worse," I said. I sniffed and wiped my nose on my arm.

The pressure of my arms and legs eventually calmed Jack down, and he slumped deeper against my body, his fight momentarily over. These tantrums, which I called "DEFCON Three," had come within twenty-four hours of starting the medication. Jack had punched or kicked holes in three walls plus a bedroom door.

At that moment, I made a decision. No more Prozac. The little boy I held wasn't himself, and I would do whatever it took to get to the bottom of his pain.

"I promise you that you are safe," I said, kissing the top of his head. "I'm here with you and won't leave." I struggled to my feet, picked him up and swung him to my hip. I could feel his birdlike bones beneath my hands. At nine years old, he ought to weigh more than fifty pounds.

Once Jack was safely settled into his bed to rest, I called Dr. H. The answering service took a message, assuring me I'd receive a return call momentarily. It took two days for him to return my call. I told him my decision.

"You're making a huge mistake. We can switch SSRIs and try another brand," Dr. H said.

"No. We'll find another way. No more medication," I said, my voice firm. I told him we no longer required his services and hung up. I felt limp. Scared. Uncertain. What if he was right? What if I was making a mistake that could harm my son? I shook off those feelings and launched into research mode.

I came upon alternative modalities and talked to Jack about them. One was acupuncture.

"Will I get stuck with needles?" Jack asked.

I assured him that needles were optional. "Acupuncture is Japanese, like Manga." I knew he'd say yes as he was obsessed with anything having to do with Japanese cartoons.

A recommendation came from a long-time family friend for a therapist named Leslie, who also had a quirky kid. We couldn't have found a better provider.

Jack felt for the first time since his diagnosis that he was in control of his health and it gave him the confidence he hadn't had before. Our bedtime routine now included rubbing lavender on his ankles and head before we read together. It worked like a charm!

During my research for holistic practitioners, I'd come across many articles supporting the elimination of gluten from spectrum kids' diets. As Jack had allergies to all grasses and all pollens, it seemed reasonable to me that removing gluten was our next step.

"Absolutely not," Jack's dad Ron said. "You can take him off gluten at your house, but I'm not going to do it."

"That's not how it works. We both have to eliminate it for at least two weeks to see if there's any difference," I said.

"You're making this up to create problems," he said. "We're not doing it here." He hung up the phone.

Stubbornness isn't one of my best qualities, but I embraced it in this fight. Jack had begun to see a "talking therapist," and I asked her if she would explore the idea of going gluten-free with him. Once the therapist told Jack's dad that Jack wanted to give it a try, a reluctant agreement was reached. Ron would do so for two weeks. But only two weeks.

I had Jack make a list of all his favorite foods. Together, we researched what was naturally gluten-free. Things that weren't, we looked for at the natural food market. Those things that we couldn't find we made. The only thing we couldn't replace was his favorite cereal. Not too shabby!

After only two weeks on this new diet, Jack gained fifteen pounds. The pediatrician was gobsmacked. Jack hadn't gained weight in over three years, but with this simple switch, he packed on the pounds. His ribs were no longer visible.

The true test came when Jack's court-appointed therapist asked him to draw what it felt like in his body to be on gluten. Jack sketched sharp, jagged lines in black and gray. On another sheet of paper, she had him create an image of what it felt like to be gluten-free. In soft pastel crayons, he drew gentle sloping lines.

Jack's dad relented, finally. I felt like a matador who safely avoided a rampaging bull. My intuition was two for two.

By this point, Jack saw weekly an occupational therapist, speech therapist, psychologist, and acupuncturist. On one of our many trips home from a therapy session, Jack asked from the backseat, "Mommy, am I broken?"

It took all my willpower not to crumble into a puddle of tears. I white-knuckled the steering wheel. "Oh, sweetie, you're perfect just as you are." At that moment, I made a radical decision: the way Jack's therapies were delivered must change, so my beautiful son never again asked such a heartbreaking question. I resigned from my high-stress corporate position as I could no longer work seventy hours a week and support Jack the way I wanted to. For the first time, I became a stay-home mom. During the day, I homeschooled Jack, and at night I studied, going so far as to become certified in a variety of autism-related support programs.

We transformed one of our bedrooms into Jack's playroom, a place where I spent at least four hours a day devoted entirely on meeting Jack right where he was, allowing him to take the lead on any games we played. We did improv using oversized pillows, told stories with puppets, drew huge pictures, built Legos, read books, and created forts. Most importantly, we connected, deeply.

If by chance his eyes met mine, I gushed, "You have the most beautiful eyes! I love when you look at me."

Slowly and over time, Jack's eye contact with me strengthened. He continued to gain weight and returned to school.

From that time forward, Jack blossomed. As a high school freshman, he led a team of artists to paint a mural in their school. As a junior, he gained admission into a prestigious animation program. Today, Jack recently graduated high school. He has been accepted into four top universities for animation and graphic design. I know in my heart that his success, while his own, was forged because I listened to my intuition and bucked norms.

Reflection

Have you ever gone against popular belief to forge your own path? What happened when you did?

____

____

____

____

What unexpected gifts did your children bring to your life? How do they help you to shine?

____

____

____

____

When was a time you chose to honor your intuition, despite contrary opinions? How did you come to that decision, and what was the result?

____

____

____

____

Chapter Two

SING YOUR OWN SONG

MY AUTHENTIC VOICE

Lizete Morais

"Come sing that song I love, Lizete," Dad called from the living room. "Your aunt is here, and I'm sure she would love to hear it."

I was sitting in my bedroom, doing my history homework. When I heard his request, I froze as the old, familiar nervousness set in. I was seventeen years old, and had loved music for as long as I could remember. It was a family joke that I started singing before I could talk, and the guitar had been a part of my world since I was six.

But … was I good enough to sing for other people?

I wasn't sure, and I didn't really have the courage to find out, so it mostly remained a mystery—except for those awkward moments when Dad insisted. My sweet dad loved my singing, but I wondered: what was he getting me into?

"So, are you coming, then?"

I jumped, startled. Dad was hanging in the doorway with a goofy smile on his face. I knew how proud he was, and of course I can't let him down. He was the youngest child in his family, and the opinions of his four older sisters were important to him—and so, of course, they became important to me.

With shaking hands, I grabbed my guitar and a piece of A4 paper on which I'd written the chords to "The Rose" by Bette Midler, and made my way to the judgment seat.

The first verse was a little shaky, but I found my groove, and by the second and third verses, I was really into it. The music took over. I forgot who and where I was, and simply dove into the essence of the song. Singing, I felt free, expansive, harmonious, and peaceful … and I was rocking it.

At the end of the song, Dad started clapping with loose abandon. Then, both of us gazed toward my aunt. My eye met hers, and I searched them for the sweet confirmation that yes, I was good enough.

Then, my aunt did something that would set my course for many years to come. She scrunched up her nose, looked me straight in the eyes, and formed a word that could only be communicated as … Meh."

My heart sank. Shame and embarrassment set in. All my fears were confirmed in that one syllable. I was not good enough to sing in public.

Years passed. I never stopped singing—but if I did raise my voice it was always behind closed doors, or in very private or intimate settings. This reflected in other areas of my life.

For as long as I can remember, I've been painfully aware of something I lovingly refer to as "The Gap." It used to permeate my every waking moment. I saw it everywhere—like when I *knew* what I wanted to say during a presentation at work, but when I actually stood up to present, it came out wobbly, as my body shook with nerves. Or, when I needed to have a delicate conversation, and my intention was clear, the words perfect in my mind—but then, the delivery would be totally different.

I felt this continuous gap for a long time, and eventually realized that The Gap was the space between who I knew I was on the inside and what actually manifested in my behavior. Needless to say, this bled into almost every area of life: my relationships, my work, my alone moments. It was so frustrating to have the dreams that I did, to feel the potential that was within me, and yet feel too crippled to truly show up.

At age nineteen, I discovered the self-development world—and it was heaven. For the first time, I didn't feel alone. All of us were fellow seekers. We all had dreams, and wanted to have an impact on the world, but we had identified that we needed to improve ourselves in one way or another to truly achieve our goals.

After fifteen years of reading every book I could, going to seminars, and earning countless certifications, my life had indeed changed. I married one of the best human beings I have ever met. I had a thriving corporate career, and was the director of training and communication for a prestigious pharmaceutical company. I was financially stable—and in the eyes of my family, I had "made it."

I should have been happy. But The Gap was still there, just as wide as ever.

The truth was, I had learnt incredibly valuable skills to help me navigate the outer world, but my inner being was just as insecure, frustrated, and unhappy as it had always been—right up until the moment that changed *everything*.

I had just finished what was considered a very productive and insightful presentation to some colleagues, and was walking towards the train station when the inner conversation of "I should have, I needed to, I could have" started for the millionth time. But this time, a new thought stopped me in my tracks:

"I just wish I could be the person I know I am within!"

This was the key. What I saw in that moment of awakening was that my entire journey of "personal development" was based on a false premise. It was based on the idea that something was missing, that something was wrong with me, that something about me needed to be different. It was a journey based on self-rejection.

What my soul showed me at that moment was that the journey of transformation wasn't about changing *me* at all. Rather, it was about discovering who I truly was before all the conditioning, limited programming, and false beliefs I held about myself took hold. The journey was completely upside down!

"But," I asked myself, "How do I truly know myself? How do I heal and recover all the parts of me that have been stolen, or forgotten, or broken?"

This question started me on a journey to find new teachers and modalities. First, I worked on my mind with neuroscience; then, I worked on my heart intelligence and intuitive knowing. I studied soul-alignment and consciousness. I started understanding that transformation takes place on five levels: mind, heart, soul, body, and energy.

Over the next three years, I completely transformed my life from the inside out. My husband and I consciously separated. I moved to a new country, and left my corporate career to become a full-time speaker, author, trainer, and coach.

Alignment doesn't always require us to change as drastically as I did—but a 180-degree shift was what I required. Although it was challenging, I wouldn't change my path for the world.

In this new chapter of life, I found myself more abundant and successful, more in love, and more accomplished than ever before. But the true beauty was that I had found peace. I felt truly happy most of the time—and when things showed up that weren't in alignment, I was quickly able to go to the core of the issue, and continue the journey of healing yet another piece of myself. I was finally on my own team! I had closed The Gap. There was no more questioning myself, no more wondering what the "right" thing to say was. I could truly live in my authenticity.

During this time, I was also creating a new body of work—one that would incorporate transformation at all five levels, and would guide other spiritually-minded and empathic women through the steps of their evolution in an accelerated way. My desire was that other women would know their truth, embody it fully, and live it abundantly. I named this body of work ARISE: Awakening, Remembering, Integration, Surrender, Emergence.

ARISE became a seven-day sacred soul retreat in 2017. It went beyond expectation and every possible imagination. I watched with awe as nine women opened up in this sacred space to find the truth within them and start putting together the pieces like never before. They shone! I shone! It felt like I had found what I'd been looking for my whole life.

On the last night of our retreat, we went to a beachside restaurant to celebrate a sacred ceremony of commitment to standing in our authentic voices. There was an artist singing, and he asked about the group I was leading. While we were chatting, he blurted, "You are a singer!"

I blushed immediately, as my old and long-buried trigger was pressed. "No! I'm not a singer. I just … sing sometimes."

As the night went on, the memory of me sitting there, shaking, in front of my disapproving aunt came flooding back. I realized that this, too, was just one of the thousands of moments when I believed in someone else's projection instead of truly knowing and loving myself. It was time to claim my magic back.

I left the dinner table and made my way determinedly toward the artist. I told him that I had a song to sing. I found the perfect song—"Angel" by Sarah McLachlan.

As the music started, I didn't hesitate. I didn't tremble or shake. I was singing for *me*. No one had to love it, or even like it. I was singing for my love of music, and for the love of my seventeen-year-old self who had done her best in that moment. I would honor her. I would see her. I would love her.

I was blown away when I looked up and saw the eyes of my

audience. Some with their mouths open. Some with tears welling in their eyes. Some shaking their heads in disbelief. Every one of them moved.

I will never stop singing. Not because now I have the confirmation that I can sing. Not because someone has given me permission. Not because others think I am "good enough." I will sing, and I will shine, because that's what my soul was born to do.

For all my sisters out there who are still haunted, or still questioning the beauty and power of their song, I say to you: Sing, sweet soul, in all your glory, uniqueness, and love. You deserve to be heard.

Reflection

Do you recall an experience where you felt you were being judged as "not good enough"? How did that experience shape your choices? How can you make a different choice now?

Is your personal development journey actually leading you to your truth, or are you in an endless cycle of "fixing" things about yourself? What can you do to embrace your true self, as you are right now?

Do you perceive a gap between what's inside you and how you move through the world? What's one thing you can do today to start showing up as the true you?

THE SUN WILL COME OUT TOMORROW

Lisa Marie Rosati-Grantham

The first time I stepped into the spotlight, I was in fifth grade. After some sing-a-longs with my choir mates (which, unbeknownst to any of us, were covert auditions), I won the singing solo for the school's winter concert. The song Ms. Hemingway chose for me to perform was "Tomorrow," the show-stopper from the musical, *Annie*.

Before that point, I had never opened my mouth to sing. I'm an introvert—a gregarious introvert, but an introvert all the same. An observer. I think I was five before I stopped watching everyone and actually started to talk. Singing was another realm altogether.

I'd love to describe for you all the feelings I experienced during my performance—but, honestly, I have zero recollection of it. Nor did I have any inkling of the epic emotional chaos that would engulf my life shortly thereafter.

I assure you, if I'd had any idea what was coming, I never would have sung that damned song.

There was a cassette recording of my performance. I remember listening to it later, hearing myself wrap up the song. There was a pause, then a huge *roar* from the audience. The cheering and whistling went on for minutes. I thought, "Why is everyone going so crazy over my singing? I had no idea I was so talented."

I landed the solo for the spring concert too—"Blue Bayou" was the song. Then, the principal of our elementary school asked me to sing "The Way We Were" for the sixth grade graduation in June. I was flattered, and felt compelled to say yes. I was a major people pleaser, and the pride that the adults around me so obviously felt was like a drug I couldn't resist. In fact, I was so focused on the fact that I was being acknowledged and celebrated that I failed to notice that the sixth grade class had started a school-wide petition against me. They did *not* want me to sing at their graduation. I'm still not sure why.

That was the first time I was at the wrong end of an angry mob. It was many against one. Going to school scared the crap out of me, and my heart broke a little more every night when my parents did absolutely nothing to protect me. My dad always did his best to avoid conflict of any kind, so there was no way he was going to go to bat on my behalf. My mom, on the other hand, asked me, "What did you do to turn them all against you?" and said things like, "If it was me in your shoes, I'd punch their lights out!"

I wanted to back out of singing the solo, but the principal begged me not to. He said that *he* wanted me to sing at the graduation, even if the whole sixth grade didn't, and would I please do it for him? A big part of me wanted to say no, but I didn't want to disappoint him or my mother—and the rebellious, badass part of me wanted to say "screw you" to the schoolmates who had so viciously turned on me.

I sang that damned solo like a pro, and then cried my eyes out publicly.

At the end of the school year, those nasty sixth-graders moved up to the junior high school, so I had eight weeks of summer vacation plus a whole academic year before I had to suffer their company again.

That experience scarred me for a long, long time. Every decision I made in regard to shining my light in the world got filtered through that lens. I held myself back for fear that I would be noticed, singled out, and picked on. Being ostracized by my peers became a recurring theme. I always felt like the odd girl out, like there was no one I could trust or rely upon. My parents' inability to create a safe environment for me underscored that. I mean, if they wouldn't even stick up for me, how could I expect to be supported by anyone else?

I thank all that is holy that, at the age of sixteen, I found my way to metaphysical books and opened myself up to spiritual concepts. Delving into mindset and the great mystery put me on a trajectory of personal growth and self-mastery that helped me begin to move through my struggles. I remember feeling so alive and hopeful when reading books by Wayne Dyer and Silver Ravenwolf. Anything and everything became possible when I was in that mindset, and I liked it—a lot.

In my late thirties, I felt called to start an online business to help women step into their personal power and magically create abundant lives and businesses they love. I started teaching the concepts and topics I'd spent so many years studying—like mindset, boundaries, and mind-body-spirit health. I was beyond inspired—and beyond afraid at the same time. I had finally come to a place where I had a circle of good friends and didn't need the approval of the masses, but the thought of flinging myself onto the world-wide web was terrifying.

Was I *crazy*?

Probably, I decided. I mean, I couldn't even handle a bunch of sixth-graders treating me like a leper. What made me think I could handle the world? That, and many other fearful thoughts, consumed me. The Goddess Lifestyle Plan® was just a twinkle in my heart, and already I was trying to talk myself out of it.

I wasn't going to let that happen.

Shining my light took massive amounts of courage, vision, determination, and grit. The Divine designed me perfectly for this task. Not only do I have tons of heart and many talents, I also have grit, determination, and tenacity. I'm the girl who got bullied—but I'm also the girl who sang anyway. Those gifts, and my willingness to see it through, carried me through my fear to a place of global impact.

What helped me most was what I like to call "F*uck it" moments. When I was afraid of internet trolls saying horrible things to me, I felt that fear deeply—and then said, "F*uck it. I've lived through this already, and I survived." That thought gave me the courage to hit "publish" every time. Throwing myself into the deep end of the pool is the best way for me to feel the fear and do it anyway.

I know now that my soul path is to be a leader, and to share my message with the women I am blessed to serve. I also know that I'll bump up against resistance over and over again, because I have chosen to lead from a place of truth. Life can be brutal and glorious, amazing and unfair—but instead of hiding the belly-flops and dark nights of the soul, I share them with my tribe, and we carry each other through.

I've also been blessed to find a safe place with the love of my life, Shannon. (It only took us fifty years to find each other!) With him, I've found trust like I've never known before. With him at my back, I can be real in every situation, whether I'm conquering the world or crying with my head under a blanket because it's all just too much.

I'd be lying if I said I've become a thick-skinned rock of a woman who can joyfully wave her middle finger at mean people and internet trolls without batting an eyelash. But the good news is that the trigger of judgment is minuscule now compared to what it used to be—and amen for that! Now, I'm excited to keep stepping onto even bigger stages in my life, and embrace the possibilities to come!

Reflection

Is there a childhood experience that has made you afraid to shine your light? How has it impacted you?

Do you have a hard time trusting others? How do you think this impacts your ability to shine in the world?

What can you do to give yourself the experience of shining on your own stage today?

MY SHINING NIGHT

Kathleen Gubitosi, MA

Sing? Did she just ask me to *sing*? My body froze yet somehow I managed to speak.

"Uh, sing, at your church?"

"Yeah, could you sing on Christmas Eve?" Joy, one of my dearest friends, was the wife of a pastor of a local church. She wanted me to be the soloist, to sing the opening song for their Christmas Eve service.

I sat in silence at my desk. Sing? Me? In public? She asked me to sing! I don't sing anymore. I should never have said anything! How do I get out of this without ruining our friendship?

I worked in banking, having reinvented myself and I never discussed why I'd abandoned my music career except to say that there were no teaching jobs, which was true. How was Joy to know it wasn't the whole truth? I couldn't take another music teaching job even if there were one.

After almost six years, I still managed chronic myofascial pain and the excruciating symptoms of temporal mandibular joint dysfunction, the results of a freak accident that turned my life upside down and destroyed my career. My lifelong dream of being a singer had evaporated.

Those first medical reports devastated me. The doctors told me my days as an entertainer were finished. I would never recover. The best outcome would be to manage the pain, get over the emotional loss of performing—professional or otherwise—and find a way to support myself in a non-musical career.

The physical pain was tortuous and emotional waves of bitterness, despair, anger, and grief consumed me. The effort—years of practice and sacrifice—all for nothing! Student loan debt. Driving my old tin can of a car. Missing parties and dates for rehearsal. They all had been a waste of time!

I kept my grief and anger hidden behind a cheerful, well-trained performer's face. Crumpling to the floor and becoming a keening mess was a luxury I couldn't afford for long. I had to start over. To survive, I squashed the artist inside me and everything that went with her—until Joy's request.

Within seconds, I said, "Joy, I don't think I can do it. I haven't sung in over five years."

"Will you think about it? We'd love it. We know you'll do a beautiful job," Joy said.

How would she know? She'd come into my life after singing had left. She'd never heard me so much as hum with the radio in the office. I backed up my reluctance with more excuses hoping she'd drop it. "I'm not sure what we're doing Christmas Eve. Let me find out what our plans are."

I avoided the question hoping it would fade off into the ether on its own. I didn't want to hurt Joy's feelings. Days passed, and I thought I was in the clear.

A few days later, she asked again, "Do you know if you can sing for Christmas?"

The wistfulness in her voice got to me. I took a deep breath and steadied myself to stick to my "No." I opened my mouth to put an end to the discussion and felt my heart twisting in my chest all over again.

I thought I was numb to the hopelessness and misery, the

maddening feeling of being cheated out of my dreams. You would think you'd be over it after almost six years. Tears welled up in my eyes. Who was I kidding? I'd never be over it!

Frustration and long-festering rage flowed through me. Inside, the five-year-old dreamer, who'd been mesmerized by Judy Garland, threw herself to the floor kicking and screaming, beating her fists into the ground. Despair and resentment won. I felt trapped mourning the death of my childhood dreams.

Then I heard her. It was the voice of my long-buried performer self! She'd resurfaced.

It's one song, not a whole concert. You don't have a voice injury. It's a musculoskeletal problem. Yeah, it'll hurt, but you're in constant pain anyway, what's the difference?

The wounded me wanted to remain safely inside my cocoon of suffering, replaying images of lying in bed, unable to hold my head up, unable to eat without pain, and unable to sit up to play the piano. Unable, unable, unable! Fear reverberated through my brain.

I found it nearly impossible to speak. Blood pounded in my head as the scars on my heart tore open in an anguished tug of war. I realized in that instant that my entire life was destined to be tainted with "what-ifs" unless I found a way to reconcile my brokenness. Joy had offered me a chance to escape my hell.

I looked at her and blurted, "Yes. I can do it."

"Great! Can you sing 'O Holy Night'?"

Oh, holy crap! My return to public singing would begin with a carol that called for vocal stamina, flexibility, and dramatic storytelling. Of course, they couldn't have picked something easy like "Silent Night"!

That weekend, I kicked myself as I scanned the shelves of karaoke tapes in the local Christian supply store. What the hell had I agreed to? I must have been crazy.

Then I saw it: "O Holy Night" labeled "for both high and low voice." One version had to work.

My ego tried to protect me and derail my commitment with thoughts of inadequacy. The ghost in my head fought dirty as I carried the cassette to the cashier. What if it's awful? What if you can't do it?

Its last-ditch effort shouted at me. "You're risking your health and sanity for a few moments of singing! What's gonna happen the day after? Do you think you're strong enough to survive this?"

I've survived so far. I can do this. I paid the cashier and left with the cassette.

Once I started rehearsing, I felt like a novice. That was the key! I needed to go back to the beginning and become a student.

My teacher's mind knew I only had to perform the song once. The rehearsals would be the real test. That was my real fear: not surviving daily practice. So, I planned strategically. Every day, I listened to the cassette on repeat. Every night, I sang the song once, recorded myself, and made notes. Both my pain and singing were awful. The sound of screeching cats would have been easier to listen to. What were you thinking? I asked myself for the millionth time.

Practice was grueling. I knew that the show must go on. My neck and shoulder muscles, hard as rocks on a regular day, became boulders. My jaw cracked, shifted, and popped. My head felt like it was in a vice. I slept with one heating pad on my neck and another on my face. I prayed for strength, for courage, for the right steps to take in practice, for the days until Christmas Eve to pass quickly, to sound good in performance, to not embarrass my friends, and not to damage myself further. Whenever fearful thoughts arose, I repeated my mantra, I've survived so far. I can do this. Those words became my lifeline.

My confidence grew with each practice run. The bigger surprise was that my love of interpreting music returned as I played the role of both teacher and student.

On Christmas Eve, I felt physically exhausted and emotionally drained from the gamut of emotions swirling within me. I had expected this. What I didn't expect was the calm poise that filled me, freeing and opening my heart—a heart able to express with certainty the sacred stillness of "O Holy Night"!

When it was time, I stood on the chancel, looked out, and saw Joy smiling at me. I sang with gratitude for the blessed opportunity to share a musical offering. My spirit soared. I felt whole again.

I had the next three days off from the bank, and I spent them lying in bed. One song wiped me out physically. Emotionally, I felt thrilled! I'd done it. Lying flat on my back and in tremendous physical pain, inside I jumped up and down. Hope lit me up. I knew that given time, practice, and more healing, singing could perhaps become a source of personal enjoyment again—even if I only sang in the shower.

It took another six years before I became strong enough to resume performing regularly, taking roles in regional theater. No longer a banker, I claimed my real title: artist. I returned to private voice coaching because a friend's daughter wanted singing lessons. My practice thrives as I do work I love.

I'm not pain-free but thanks to Joy's question, my relationship with music and voice has broadened in ways I could never have dreamed of and brought the most beautiful people and experiences into my life. I am truly grateful.

Reflection

What have you told yourself you couldn't do, even though you desperately wanted to? How have these messages affected your life?

Think back to a time when you were hurt, either physically or emotionally. How did you respond? What did you learn from the experience?

What sacrifices have you made to achieve your goals?

Chapter Three

GO YOUR OWN WAY

MOVE INTO FREEDOM

Monica Dubay

I am sitting in the office of the divorce mediator in Newark, New Jersey. I have made an important decision: to leave my husband of fourteen years, and leave the state to start my life over. I want to take my two boys, ages five and eight, with me when I go.

This moment will determine whether or not I can actually do it.

In seventeen years, I have never insisted that my needs be heard. I don't know how to ask. And yet, here I am, asking.

I'm not sure why I think there's any chance that my husband will grant me something so challenging to his comfortable life, so disruptive to our family's status quo. I pray for his understanding, but I'm facing his anger and his need to control. I'm challenging the idea that I need to stay in my place as a wife and mother, and keep swallowing my pain, loneliness, disconnection, and desire for freedom.

I feel like prayer isn't enough. I need a miracle.

I know this will affect all of us deeply, and I am terrified. I want to do this for myself, but it's likely that he will stop me. My lawyer has advised me that it's not a good idea to try to take the kids out of state. But I am willing to try, because I have a vision.

I have just turned forty. My life is begging to open up through decisive action. I almost don't recognize myself. I found a spiritual program in Wisconsin, and a center where people are dedicated to living their desire for awakening, healing, and transformation. I visited last summer. I connected with the other participants on so many levels. I know it is where I am meant to be.

I felt freer than ever before in Wisconsin. People there "got me"; they knew who I was, and what I was feeling, because they were on the same path. I felt like I had finally come home. And yet, the idea of making such a huge change left me distraught.

I took a long walk along the lake and kept asking myself, how will I do this? Should I do it? My kids need their dad, they will be so affected by this … how will I live? How will I make money?" My thoughts swirled. But then, as I walked along, I heard an unmistakable inner voice say distinctly, "If you move here, you will be happy forever."

That was the day I called my husband and told him I was filing for divorce. He wasn't surprised—but he did say something to the effect of, "The kids have to stay with me."

Now, a few months later, we are sitting in the mediator's office, and I am praying for a miracle.

The mediator is very polite. She reminds me of my older sister, who is like a second mother to me. She is very calm as she turns to me and says, "You've been alone all these years, haven't you?" I burst into tears.

For seventeen years, my husband worked every night until midnight or later in a music recording studio. I had to live with this, no matter how much I pleaded with him to change his schedule. I felt like I was always alone, unsupported, ignored.

I don't expect the divorce to be easy on any of us. That's why I've been putting it off for years. Who am I to ask for what I want? And yet, I know that if I don't go, if I don't do this, my life will go right back to being controlled by him and my staunch Catholic upbringing. I can't accept that.

The mediator asks, "What do you want to do?"

I tell her what I want: to move to Wisconsin and take our boys with me. My soon-to-be ex shakes his head. He doesn't want me to go.

"I'd like to speak to your husband alone," the mediator says. I leave the room, shaking.

I go into another office and sit alone. Feelings of anger, of rage, surface. Will he control my life, even after divorce? What's the point of all of this if I don't get to be free? All of my doubts flood into my mind at once.

Feeling helpless, sobbing, I begin to pray. "Please help me!" I was so frustrated. I have lived this way for too long. At the same time, I'm battling the shame of not being like other mothers, who suck it up and "stay together for the kids." I'm not happy, and I want more. Is that wrong?

Through my tears, I look around the room ... and I see it.

There, in the corner, is a simple cardboard box. It reads, "Wisconsin Paper."

It's a sign. Everything is going to be okay. I might not know the outcome, but that box gives me hope. More, it reminds me of a dream I had three years ago.

In that dream, I was living with a partner who was not my husband. He was on the same spiritual path as me. It felt so real, so amazing because I was so happy. When I woke up, I realized that this was not only possible, but probable. It scared me. I told my husband about the dream, and began to pray for the reconciliation of our marriage.

For three years, I hung on. For a while, it worked. We went to counseling. We bought and fixed up a house in the suburbs, which gave us a lot more room. I hoped that he could work from home. But no matter how much I asked, our life didn't really change, and

I resigned myself to living alone with the kids all week, only seeing him on the weekends.

Now, we are here.

I don't want to take our boys from him, but I can see no other way. I have been there for our kids full-time since the days they were born, and they are bonded to me. I can't imagine living without them.

The mediator calls me back into the room, and says to my husband, "Monica is moving to Wisconsin. That issue is closed. Now, what are we going to do about the boys?"

No discussion. Just fact.

I take a breath. This is really happening. My life is about to change drastically. I am going to be free. I know it won't be easy, but I still find myself smiling through my tears.

We work it out so that the boys can be with their dad on all vacations and one weekend a month. I will receive enough child support and alimony to be able to survive until I work things out. I am even able to buy another house in Wisconsin. My kids will have two places to call home.

A few months later, I am packing the moving van, elated to be setting off on a brand new adventure. I see myself leaving a sad, lonely life for one of expansion and connection. I am completely elated that things have changed so drastically in such a short period of time. It's a miracle of grace. By stepping into the unknown, I have found a way to be free.

***

Today, I celebrate my choice for freedom. My kids have grown into beautiful young men. They did go back to live with their father after a long custody battle that rocked our world and made them who they are—but I know now, that my choice for freedom actually helped them to become more compassionate and loving.

I will always be grateful for that mediator who saw who I was and what I needed. I'm also grateful for the earth angels along the way who guided me and showed me that my feelings matter—that I matter. I have learned to forgive my ex-husband and put the past behind us. I have let go of the resentment I carried for so long, because that story is over. It ended when I gave up hanging onto it, and freed myself from its shackles.

Today, my work is to help others shift out of their own stuck places, so that they can claim their lives of freedom from pain and suffering. I help them move into their zone of genius, to live lives of self-love and service to others, take the risks that really matter, and bring their inner light forward—just as I did.

Reflection

Do you have a vision for freedom in your life?

Where are you allowing your fear of the unknown to keep you trapped?

What can you do to bring your old story to a close and let go of resentment toward those you perceive as having held you back?

RAISING THE BAR

Felicia Baucom

On the night of my seventeenth birthday, my father made me a cake. He was in an unusually good mood, so I used this evening as an opportunity to talk about college. Instead of a conversation, I was met with immediate blowback. "We already talked about this! Why are you asking about this *again*?"

Later, in a much calmer tone, he explained that my teachers were pressuring me to go to college right away when I didn't need to. In reality, he just wanted me to wait. He said, "You will do what pleases me and your mother."

As an Air Force family, we were stationed in England during my last two years of high school. At the beginning of my senior year, everyone was talking about college plans back in the States. My parents praised my intelligence and honor roll status to anyone who would listen, but since they weren't going back to the States for another two years, they intended my plans to coincide with theirs.

I went along with his agenda, even though I didn't understand it. I was conflicted: I wanted to go to college, in part, because all the kids were doing it, and in part because I was a high-achiever who wanted to keep going with my education. In addition, my entire life had involved changing schools—I had attended seven different schools over the course of twelve years, so the idea of staying put for four years excited me.

For the most part, I made the best of my situation. I spent the year after graduation working in the stereo department at the Base Exchange, representing Sony Electronics. I sold a lot of televisions, since they were one of the first things Americans bought when they moved to Europe. I used some of those funds to travel to France and the Netherlands, and made frequent trips to London with friends.

Despite all the fun I had, I continued to feel the tension between satisfying my need to continue my education and pleasing my parents. My desires won in the end. I researched colleges in the southeastern U.S. and made plans. I shared my thoughts about going to college near one of my grandmothers, hoping that would ease my parents' concerns about being on my own. My father wasn't thrilled, even tried to convince me to wait a while longer. But my mother understood, and with her support, I moved forward and flew back to the States.

I was excited and uncomfortable at the same time; I wished I had my father's full approval, but I couldn't wait to be on my own. The discomfort eased over time, especially when I reunited with my tiny but feisty grandmother and her '77 Buick at the airport. My grandmother hadn't always been free to make her own decisions, so she was eager for me to go to college to experience what she couldn't. It also helped to meet new people and embrace the college life I had heard so much about from my high school friends and the media.

Four years later, I graduated with honors—and shortly thereafter, people began to give me advice for my future, starting with, "Don't get too big for your britches." It was a family member who said it, but it could have easily been my boyfriend at the time, or one of my sociology classmates, or the manager at my first job out of college. Over time, I heard the same mantra from other friends, and even someone I met at a Monkees concert meet-and-greet. Throughout the first few years, I held positions in sales, training, administration, and technical support. With every job, there was at least one person who figuratively stood there with their arms folded, judging me for my choices.

I took on their feelings as if they were mine. I believed that if I behaved a certain way and kept my thoughts and feelings to myself, eventually they'd get over their issues and see me for who I really was. *Then* I'll have full permission to show my brilliance. *Then* I could shine like a supernova. *Then* I could move around my life the way I wanted to.

Yet they continued to judge me. In my role as a trainer, I often traveled out of town to work with clients, so I didn't have to show up at an office every day. However, those who were always there referred to me as a "slacker," and said things like, "Who do you think you are, showing up at 3:00 p.m.?" What they didn't see was how demanding some clients could be, and how I was putting all my energy into my role as a trainer.

Everyone had input about my personal life. At the time, I lived with a boyfriend. Being in the South, it wasn't difficult to encounter someone who voiced their disapproval about "living in sin." In my mind, this was confirmation that I didn't know how to live my own life, and that my achievements didn't matter. I saw that no matter what I did or didn't do, someone found fault. Someone found a reason to try to shut me down.

My tendency was to hunker down and hide, to complain, or resign myself to the belief that I was "too much." I played small to be safe, particularly at work, in romantic relationships, and with friends. I tried not to offend others, and if I did, I'd try to recover quickly and explain my real intentions, promising never to be so brazen again. That way, the critical ones couldn't snicker amongst themselves and evaluate my choices.

But I wanted to make a change. I had a desire to create something new—so I did. I changed jobs, moved across the country, and traveled without anyone's blessing but my own.

My most recent desire was to go on a retreat to the island of Ibiza. I was nervous to tell my husband because I know he doesn't like to spend money. As I expected, a wave of horror spread across his face as he said "No!" Immediate pushback. My initial reaction was similar to the shame and discomfort I felt when my late father reacted to my question about going to college. In the twenty-plus years since the birthday incident, I've been to hell and back in so many ways: broken relationships, being laid off or outright fired, dealing with rejection while trying to achieve a goal or realize a dream. I convinced myself that I was wrong for wanting what I want. I wasn't going to do that any longer. Over the years, many retreat opportunities have come and gone, but this one called to me.

I'd backed down with my father, but I didn't back down with my husband. Like my father, he has a strong presence. But I was no longer seventeen years old, and I was not going to let this yearning to travel go, even in the presence of immense fear. Despite his protests about the cost of airfare, I explained to my husband why it was important for me to explore, and how this retreat would help my business.

After he reluctantly agreed to the idea, I began to feel more confident about asking for what I want and following through with my desires instead of talking myself out of them. To start, I chose to focus on the excitement and adventure of visiting a new country and taking up space at a nourishing retreat. I felt empowered by prioritizing my desires over my husband's doubts and fears. Suddenly, I realized that I had been choosing myself all along; I just hadn't noticed that I had.

I chose myself when I went to college, where I created the space I needed to navigate the world my way and trust my decisions.

I chose myself in my job as a trainer and learned to let go of other's opinions. As much as reasonably possible, I focused on achieving the balance I needed, recognizing that no one was going to encourage me. I also gained the strength to stand up for myself about my choices.

I chose myself in my marriage. Instead of clamping down my passion for a free-spirited life, I raised the bar by reinforcing, even if only for myself, that my needs are just as valid as my husband's.

When I choose myself, I tap into my inherent worth. I listen to my heart as well as my brain, even when it's not always clear why. I follow the path that feels joyful and exciting, even if it's scary, unusual, or … expensive.

In choosing myself, I lovingly prioritize my needs, preferences, and aspirations over other people's fears, stories, and insecurities. When I listen to my desires, I'm full of energy and I shine.

No one is going to allow me to shine but myself. I can strive for others' permission or approval, and try to convince them that I'm worthy, but that has never worked. When I give myself permission, I become more aligned with my adventurous, creative, irreverent and curious self, which in turn allows me to live even more of my truth.

When I choose myself, I am declaring my desires. From there, the space opens. I walk through it, and shine.

Reflection

Have you ever chosen something different than what your heart wanted because of family or cultural expectations? Where did that choice lead you?

Felicia had a repeating pattern of thinking she was "wrong" for wanting what she wanted. Do you have a similar pattern in your life? How can you own your truth and stand your ground when it comes to your growth?

Are you still waiting for permission or approval to shine in your life? How can you give yourself the permission you've been waiting for?

UNMASKING MYSELF

Nicole Meltzer

Peacekeeper. Entertainer. Confidante. Helper. Good girl. Bad girl. Pretty girl. Happy girl. "Yes" girl. Each one a part of my collection of masks.

For most of my life, I wore these masks, unaware that I wore and changed them multiple times a day. In fact, I don't remember a time in my life where I didn't don a mask. That's how out of touch I was with myself.

The first mask I acquired was a "beautifully serene and pleasant to look at" mask—the face of an angel, a perfect child who didn't require a lot of fuss or care. My birth was quick and easy. I slept through the night. I didn't disturb anyone. On the outside, the mask may have appeared pretty, but inside was riddled with scars and the darkness of abandonment. My parents had separated just before I was born, so from birth, I tried on masks to manage expectations. I had to make sure the people around me loved me and stayed. So I chose to be easy. Accommodating. Not bothersome.

The next mask I created was the porcelain doll. One of my earliest memories of time spent with my father had us sitting on the couch in his office. My skirt fanned out around me, my hands folded neatly on my lap. I wore shiny shoes, frilly socks, and a bright smile. My cheeks hurt from holding that smile. But I loved the energy I received when people came into his office and commented on what a perfect little girl I was. So quiet. So pretty. So polite.

Next came the studious mask for the brilliant, going places girl. This mask received different energy than the porcelain doll. When I wore this one, I experienced the rush of special privileges—like one big hall pass—bestowed upon the worthy students at the school. Even when I didn't put effort into assignments, I still received high marks.

Wearing the studious mask had its downsides: I became less attractive to boys. And in my teenage years, the boys' attention quickly became the surrogate to my original need for my father's attention. Daddy issues at their best! That's when my downward spiral began.

When the high of "getting away with it" wore off, a new identity remained: the fraud. As I watched classmates struggling to understand calculus, I felt like I was missing something. How did I find it so easy? Perhaps my marks were just a fluke. The fraud mask quickly gave birth to the tutor mask. I felt that I needed to prove that I was smart. By helping others with their work, I received validation. I was needed, which meant people wouldn't leave me.

Every day, I vacillated between masks. My high school days incubated the version of me I would later take out into the world as an adult. A mixture of different personalities, emotions, and social roles that left me feeling like I didn't belong anywhere.

The seed planted by my experiences with my family took sprout. On the weekends with my father, I existed in the world of big yachts, fast cars, and partying. He taught me the importance of enjoying life, being free, and how money is an energy that should make life more comfortable.

My home life with my mother was more stable and low key. She taught me the importance of budgeting, focused work, and dedication as I watched her climb the corporate ladder, slow and steady. I learned priceless lessons from both parents and now live my own life as a mishmash of both sets of values. But at that time, the juxtaposition of my parents' careers and lifestyle experiences left me feeling like I straddled two worlds. I carried this into the social structure of high school, moving between the geeks, the cool kids, the Mods, the jocks, and everyone in between.

No one saw the whole Nicole, including me. But I didn't know any better. I thought this was how life was and how I was supposed to navigate it. As long as people smiled and seemed happy in my company, I figured I was mastering life—until I wasn't anymore.

Fast forward to a few years ago where I'm a mom of two young boys, a wife to a true life partner, a daughter-in-law to an elderly woman in the late stages of Alzheimer's, an only child with parents who aren't getting younger, a business owner, and a friend. I honestly felt blessed to live the life I led. Love and laughter filled my home, and my business was in alignment with my passions. And, yet, I still played the mask game.

The game ended one morning in early 2015 when I couldn't get out of bed. And I don't mean figuratively. I mean literally. I didn't have the energy to lift myself up. My husband had to carry me to the washroom and then put me back to bed. Being cared for this way was not something I envisioned for myself at age forty! I had no idea what was wrong with me. I just wanted to sleep and shut the world out. My pitcher was empty. And I couldn't bear to put on a mask that made everyone around me feel better. I later realized I had adrenal fatigue. Ironically, my need for deep sleep was my wake up call. Things needed to change, and they needed to change immediately.

My journey to uncovering all the masks I wore began that day. I learned to say no. I learned the importance of boundaries. I learned that it was okay to disappoint people (truthfully, this one I'm still working on). With each new lesson, my pitcher slowly began to fill back up.

The biggest lesson I have learned in the past three years is the freedom and power of vulnerability. I had held onto the need to be perfect from those early years of wanting everyone to be happy with me and not leave me. An interesting side effect of letting go of the perfection was the elimination of the silos I built in my life. Very rarely did I bring my various gifts together.

In business, people either came to me for the specific modality I offered or my meditation circles. One benefited from my analytical and therapeutic side while the other my energetic and spiritual side. In my personal life, most people were siloed similarly. Only those with whom I felt secure saw all sides of me. I wasn't living authentically.

After my pitcher dried up, I had no energy to hide behind my masks. I discarded them by being vulnerable—and the more vulnerable I became, the more my two sides merged. And, yes, some people left my life. Some losses hurt, triggering old abandonment feelings. But for the most part, I felt freer.

Being more vulnerable has deepened all of my relationships. The more vulnerable I am with my husband, the deeper our love blossoms. He has given me the gifts of realizing that not all men leave and I can be loved unconditionally. Every day, I am honored by waking up next to him, spending a day creating our life together, and falling asleep in his arms. This is not the kind of life that was modeled to me growing up, but it was one of which I dreamt! Now it's my reality.

I can say now that I have friends who get me, who know me, who feel me, and with whom I enjoy a reciprocal relationship of uplifting support. I am blessed to be part of a powerful group of entrepreneurial women. Within this group, I have been able to explore, in a vulnerable way, my gifts, and shine my light in a way I never have before in business. Fearlessly. Authentically.

No longer do I hide my ninja skills of being able to see the metaphors in people's lives to help them become unstuck and shine their light. Nor do I hide my intuitive skills that help people find practical ways to harness the power of the moon cycles and phases. I own it. I shine it. This is me, whole and mask-free.

Reflection

What kinds of masks do you wear? How do you think they serve you?

Messages we receive in childhood about our "perfectness" or "prettiness" or "ladylike-ness" have a way of permeating our adulthood. How has this shown up in your life?

What is your definition of authenticity? How aligned is your current life to this definition?

REDEFINING SUCCESS

Maribeth Decker

As a kid, I just wanted to be like my mom. Vivacious. Outgoing. Successful. Well, I wanted the accolades I believed came with her nursing and teaching career, but I didn't want to be a nurse. Instead, I wanted to be loved and accepted while enjoying all the perks of leadership: a big office, loads of respect, and money.

I believed this kind of life would be out of reach for me as an introvert and deep thinker with a quiet voice who lacked confidence. I lived in a world where loud, strongly-held opinions got peoples' admiration. But if I could be like my mom, I'd be valuable. I could be somebody. I'd be successful.

Growing up, I became an extremely quiet kid who easily got good grades, loved to read, and enjoyed hanging around the creek and fields near my house. I say 'became' because I remember being a saucy girl of five who kissed her boyfriend, Jack, in the back seat of her parent's car—and loved it! At eight, I adored being on stage, in the limelight.

But as I grew older, I found that my humor and insights were often unappreciated. I thought too much and too deeply, noticing when things didn't make sense. My parents called my behavior talking back, a major sin in the sixties. Schoolteachers and religious teachers were not interested in debating what they were teaching. My cousins called me an "egghead," and it wasn't a term of endearment. I was bright but not beloved. I decided to protect myself by withdrawing.

Even though I had closed down to people, God interacted with me when I was twelve. I marched into the woods and asked God, "Do you exist?" I received a crystal clear answer! I felt God withdrawing from the universe and was overcome by a deep fear and dismay as if all the air had been sucked out of the world. I thought I might die from the loneliness, the emptiness. But then God returned with all colors, warmth, and love. I never had another doubt that God was present, accessible, and had a deep, personal love for me.

The problem was that I didn't know what to do with it. The only people I knew who'd had a personal experience of the Creator were dead saints—and none of those saints had lived in my hometown of Buffalo, New York. So I kept this incredible experience to myself, hidden from others.

As college loomed, my thoughts about career once again rose. I still craved the kind of success my mother enjoyed and believed the medical field was where I belonged. I decided to become a psychiatrist, and double majored in psychology and pre-med. Despite excelling in my undergraduate coursework, my medical school applications were turned down. Not only was I dashed by this rejection, I felt humiliated and upset; I had been sure this was what I was meant to do!

What's a girl to do when she doesn't get into medical school? She joins the Navy, of course! Because I was a college graduate, I entered the Navy as an officer. My first duty station was in Puerto Rico. After surviving the Blizzard of '77, going there was an easy sell. My dad, who had been a Navy Petty Officer, glowed with pride.

Military leadership training drilled into me that, to succeed, you set goals and then achieved them. Every success came down to hard work and willpower. I set my first Naval goal: to make Commander. The fates aligned with this vision as I was selected to attend the Naval Postgraduate School and received the Chief of Naval Operations Award for Academic Excellence. I had this!

After a couple of rough tours, my dreams were dashed again. I would not make Commander. Feeling sick to my stomach, I believed that my career screeched to an end. Success felt elusive. I consoled myself that at least I had a loving husband, Winston, two young kids, and two wonderful dogs.

When we had married thirteen years earlier, Winston left the Navy. He wanted to be home, not at sea, when the kids came along. He was the first husband to join the "Yokosuka Officers' Wives' Club" in Japan, and the women changed the name to the "Officers' Spouses' Club" to make him feel welcome. He was that kind of guy.

After retiring from the Navy, I landed an administrative job and immediately set my eyes on a senior staff position, which required long hours and traveling. Sure enough, I made director and knew I was finally on my way to being successful. God, though, had other plans for me.

One morning in July 1998, as I was upstairs getting myself ready for work and the kids ready for school, Winston called to me from downstairs. I heard a large thump as if someone had dropped something heavy, like a big bag of birdseed.

"Winston!" Half dressed, I raced downstairs. My ten-year-old son Pat dashed along behind me.

Winston lay face down in the doorway between our dining room and kitchen. Pat and I turned him over. I panicked when I saw him struggling to breathe. My immediate thought was that he must be choking. Pat called 9-1-1 as I opened Winston's mouth to see if anything was lodged in his throat.

"Crap!" I thought, panicking even more if that was possible. Nothing was there.

Thankfully, the ambulance and police arrived quickly as they had been right up the street. The police officer peppered me with questions. Then a neighbor came over and took me upstairs to finish dressing. She also ushered Pat and Andrea, who was eight, out of the room as the paramedics worked on Winston. He wasn't choking; he'd had a massive heart attack. They were unable to revive him.

Within an hour, I became a single mom to two young children who had witnessed their dad die. It slowly dawned on me: it was up to me to be both parents for Pat and Andrea. No more long hours, very little traveling.

I wish I were a better person, but a part of me was crushed. I knew my version of success—promotions, people working for me, cool titles, and a big office with windows—was out of reach. That door slammed shut loud and hard!

I chose to put my kids first. Before that, I'd operated on automatic pilot: "I'm a mother. I love my kids, they're going to be great!" After Winston died, being a good mother became a conscious choice. Duty is not a word you hear much. But I felt that I had a sacred duty to my kids, to give them the best chance possible for a good life despite losing their beloved father.

In surrendering to the gift hidden in Winston's death, I found myself placed on an intuitive path. Dreams started coming fast and furious. I repeatedly dreamed that Winston returned, ready to start parenting again, not knowing he was dead. I had to gently explain he had died and he would have to take care of the kids from Heaven. I dove into clearing out the hurt and finding the light. I vividly felt Winston watching over the kids. I studied Reiki, became a master, and learned energy healing techniques.

Then the craziest thing happened after I became a Reiki Master—my dogs started communicating with me! Two of them made their presence known after they died. Timmie showed up in my dining room as a full body apparition! Later, I'd had to put Eddy down just before flying to a business meeting. She accompanied me in spirit on my plane trip to Colorado. Her strong and comforting presence allowed me to function through the meeting.

My rescue dog, Tibor, a beautiful German Shepherd/Shar Pei mix, gave me the final push to become a professional animal communicator. When I sat on the couch next to him, I would routinely see an image of a German Shepherd attacking a man wearing a bulky suit. I figured out it was time to listen to my dogs and undertook training to learn how to communicate with animals and discuss problematic behaviors, provide energy healing for body and emotional issues, and help them transition.

Animal communication helped me redefine success in such a satisfying way. Success now means unapologetically expressing and using my whole self in service to others. My intelligence, inquiring mind, warm heart, loud laugh, the joy of teaching and sharing, bawdiness, courage, intuitive abilities, incredible life experiences, slightly subversive sense of humor, and my honest sharing of imperfection are *all* necessary for my work with animals and their people.

As I dare to share my authentic self, my intuitive gifts continue to blossom. My friend Psychic Bob even told me that my Mom, who has passed, was fascinated with my energy healing. She loved how I turned out! I didn't expect that.

Reflection

How did your parents influence your ideas and thoughts about who you ought to be?

In what ways did your gifts reveal themselves?

What losses have changed the trajectory of your life? How?

Chapter Four

TRUST YOUR INNER KNOWING

NICE

Crystal Cockerham

Nice. She called me nice.

That was it. Nice. "Who calls someone nice, anyway? Nothing before or after it, just *nice*," I thought as I tossed and turned, trying to sleep. "I am so much more than nice!"

Never mind that I wasn't sure what "more than nice" meant.

Earlier that evening, as I sat in a wisdom circle, Sally, one of my fellow circle members, said I was nice. I believed she meant it as a compliment, but something about that word left me feeling angry and frustrated.

Sleep eventually came, but at some point, I jolted awake. I distinctly heard a loud voice in my head say, "You *are* more than nice. You are *so many things,* and you will never be known by them if you don't *wake up*!"

Why had this word gotten under my skin? What was wrong with being nice? Tears streamed down my cheeks. As I got up from the bed, an image came to me, and I understood why I felt like an empty shell of a woman with the word nice stamped on her with a space-age font. It seemed perfect for the robotic way I felt.

Memories flashed in my mind's eye of the long nights spent at the hospital sitting by my daughter's bedside, watching her as she moved in and out of sleep. Her nurse had advised me to stay positive regardless of how terrified and angry I felt. Not only was I utterly terrified of losing my daughter, but I was furious with the medical system for not figuring out what was wrong after months of doctor's visits. There were countless referrals to the emergency room because she was beyond office treatment. Endless doctor appointments. Extended hospitalizations. Rounds of tests. Allergic reactions to medications. These were compounded by the hospital's inability to accommodate her food allergies.

I unconsciously put intense pressure on myself as though it were my fault that my little girl struggled, that she was sick. At one point, I completely lost my cool and insisted on a new team of doctors, even though she was so weak she couldn't even keep sips of water down.

I felt so alone through that experience, wholly consumed by monitoring and caregiving. I had nothing left to give to anyone else or myself. I forced myself to steal away to have one-on-one time with my other two children. There were days that I was so physically, mentally, and emotionally exhausted that I don't even remember them.

I survived on auto-pilot, becoming an empty shell of a person because it was the only way I could stay positive. On the surface, I appeared nice, while underneath turmoil reigned. I willed my daughter's survival because the fear of losing her was paralyzing and intense.

Thankfully, my daughter eventually improved. Although she had a couple of setbacks, nothing was as terrible as those dark months where I struggled to get through the day.

Two years had passed between my daughter's illness and the night Sally declared me "nice." While I no longer felt angry or frustrated, I often wept. Why did I feel so sad? Shouldn't I feel better? I didn't know that I had stuck emotions. I just knew something was off. Then I had a realization: I had been so caught up in caretaking that I had lost myself!

At that moment, I knew that I was re-living the pain and fear of those desperate months. Being called nice forced emotions and memories to resurface. Tears flowed so I could let it all go: the doing, the fear, and the pain. Being called nice unlocked all I'd tucked deep inside.

The next day, I phoned Sally to share with her the epiphany that had arrived in the middle of the night. I couldn't wait two weeks until our next group meeting. I told her my reaction to being called nice and how it had churned up all kinds of feelings and memories. I expressed gratitude for her inciting remarks, which prompted my self-analysis.

At our next wisdom group meeting, I shared my epiphany as tears streamed down my cheeks. I'd thought myself cried out, but I was wrong. There were tears for what I'd been through, tears from what I missed because I'd been an empty husk, tears for who I no longer was, tears for being unsure of who I was, and tears for who I wanted to be. The catharsis changed me.

I spent the next year moving forward and transforming. Along with my wisdom group, I participated in a spiritual coaching program. Every tool I learned, I repeatedly used on myself. It was a year of brutal self-examination and processing. I woke up knowing I was much more than nice. I refused to allow fear to put me back to sleep.

Oh, but I struggled with fear! Once my eyes opened, and my awareness heightened, I could no longer hide from it. I had all the fears: of not being enough, of not being good enough, of not knowing myself, even of getting to know myself. Fear stalked me from the past, at work, and at home. I even had a fear of losing control, which made sense as control had gotten me through my daughter's illness and recovery. I had mastered the art of control to avoid falling apart.

It became apparent to me that, until that point, I hadn't fully comprehended what it meant to be *awakened.* I also discovered during this time that I was an empath. And guess what? I had to learn to control it. (What irony that I needed to relinquish control, yet had to control this gift for my sanity!)

As I grew, I noticed the possibilities I had to choose from and knew I had much more to learn. So much had improved by then: my work environment was healthier, things at home got better, and we found steady financial ground again. Despite learning so much in the coaching program, something was strangely missing.

It's true that the universe conspires to give you what you need to heal and grow. Within weeks, I was introduced to both a nine-month transformational program centered around the Divine Feminine Mysteries and a Crystal Healer Certification. I immersed myself in the crystal healing course during the first trimester of the transformational program. I discovered my Avalon and finally came home to myself.

I am awake, and I am home. I am a woman, whole and beautiful. I am a sacred container full of love and compassion. I am guided by the wisdom of my inner light. I am perfectly imperfect. I am here, I am home, and I am *awake*.

Nice.

Reflection

What words trigger deep emotional responses in you? Why do you think this is, and how do you handle these responses?

What impacts have you experienced in caring for a sick relative? What lessons did you take away from that situation?

In what ways do you exert control? Examine the root cause associated with that control.

THE RIGHT CLASS

Felicia D'Haiti

"I'm sorry, dear," Sister Pieta, the assistant principal and scheduler, began when she called me over summer break. "Chemistry and Human Physiology are being offered at the same time. Chemistry is a requirement, but we have a new class you might like. It's called 'Humanities.'"

"Humanities?" I thought. "What's that?"

Sr. Pieta explained that the Humanities class would examine art, music, and other cultural histories beginning with ancient cultures. It didn't sound as interesting as Human Physiology, but I reluctantly agreed to try it.

I had wanted to be a nurse, and then a doctor, since elementary school. While I didn't love math and science (especially not math), I had worked hard to understand and make progress in those areas so that I could stay on my future career path. Little did I know that my enrollment in that Humanities class—and my future relationship with its teacher—would have a major impact on my life path.

On the first day of school, I sat begrudgingly in my new class, and contemplated why I was one of only three juniors in a class of all seniors. I remembered the Humanities teacher visiting my English class the previous year to talk about this new class and encourage us to sign up for it. I also recall thinking at the time that I would never in a million years take this class. It served no purpose for me.

That same teacher glided into the classroom. Tall, slender, dressed in a long, flowing skirt, she was full of passion for her subject, and so confident. She was also determined to make sure we were culturally aware and didn't "walk around like awkward, ignorant tourists." She demanded that we act like—and become—cultured, proper young women who were aware of their cultural histories, especially in art. She made it "not cool" not to know.

The course and its contents, especially our studies of Ancient Egypt, fascinated me. During that class, a passion for art history and the arts in general was ignited within me.

We went to museums, plays, ballets, and other dance performances, and on longer trips to New York City. I will never forget visiting the ancient Egyptian temples in the Metropolitan Museum of Art. Finally, I had found something that I loved to talk about, read about, and learn about. I felt so differently about this content. It wasn't like math or science, where I was interested but not passionate.

I loved the class so much that I tried to take it again the following year. When it wouldn't fit into my schedule, I tried to talk Sr. Pieta and the administration into an independent study. When that didn't work, I just continued to spend time with my favorite teacher and talk about art history and other topics.

When it came time to apply to colleges, I briefly mentioned to my parents that I was considering changing my direction from medicine to art history. After receiving an overwhelmingly negative reaction, especially from my mother, I dropped the discussion. I thought it would be better to keep the peace and compromise. I discovered that it was, in fact, possible to be a pre-med art history major, so that's what I did. Yet, with this decision, I felt constricted. Did I still want to be a medical doctor, or did I want to pursue my new passion?

During my first semester in college I felt so detached from the math and science courses. Every day became a struggle. That's when I truly discovered how little passion I had for the topics, and how I had only tolerated them because I saw them as necessary if I wanted to become a doctor.

I didn't like feeling stuck, so I started asking questions and began to explore my options. I spoke with some of the art history professors. I researched careers in various fields, all the while loving my art history classes and lamenting the torture of being bored to death in botany and calculus.

During my explorations, I was encouraged to speak with different advisors on campus, but after receiving negative reactions from two of them, I stopped asking questions. Apparently, it was the collectively-held opinion that I shouldn't release my pre-med studies because there were not enough minorities in the sciences. They were beginning to sound like my mother. I felt as if they didn't want me to be happy, but just wanted me to do what was expected. On the other hand, the professors and staff in the art history department were welcoming and encouraging. They helped me to make connections with former graduates who were working in area galleries and museums, and pointed me toward resources. I even managed to get a job in the art history department, rotating between the art gallery, the slide library, and the front office.

After a semester of intense exploration and research, I had made my decision—at least internally. I wanted to follow my passion in my studies, and work in a museum as an art curator—ideally at the Smithsonian Institution.

When I was home for Christmas break, I decided that it was time to tell my parents. Just the thought of their reactions tied my stomach up in knots. I had said since I was in elementary school that I was going to be a doctor. They were so proud of me—and they were paying for my education. I was terrified to disappoint them. I created awful scenarios in my mind about what their reactions would be, and worked myself up into a stressed-out mess. When I finally worked up the courage to tell my dad, I could practically feel my heart beating in my throat as I spoke.

"I'm not going to continue on the pre-medicine track, Dad," I told him. "I'm not going to be a doctor."

In a calm voice, my dad responded, "I already knew that. I just want you to do what makes you happy."

I was so relieved. This was great.

Now, I just had to speak to my mother.

Her reaction was more in line with what I had anticipated. In fact, she sounded just like my advisors at school. There was a barrage of questions, like, "What will you do with that kind of degree? What kind of money will you make? What kind of life will you have?" Question after question crushed my spirit in that moment. I was dragged down by a mixture of disappointment and anger, feeling like my mother did not trust my judgment.

But … did *I* trust my judgment? I knew how I felt about my studies, and I had done the research about my possible career paths. Yet, her reaction made my doubt my choices.

My doubts didn't last long, though. Once I re-immersed myself in my studies and re-engaged with my art community, I regained the confidence in my choice even though it caused a great deal of conflict with my mother. In order to avoid the arguments, I just didn't talk about it—which led me to feel like I was hiding something, or like I had something to be ashamed of. Neither feeling was enough to make me change my mind.

That summer, I was granted an internship in the Prints and Photographs Division of the Library of Congress. I was determined to show my mother (and myself) that there were many options in the world for me, especially since we lived so close to so many museums. Over the next few years, I took advantage of every opportunity given to me to explore careers and studies in art history.

I soaked in everything. I even spent a year attending college in Fiesole, Italy. That year, I was in heaven. I adored seeing so much of the artwork that I had studied still in its original locations, still intact after hundreds of years. It was there that I fully embraced my passion for art history and let that part of myself shine without doubt, fear, or conflict.

During my work in museums after graduation, I discovered a connection between the art and objects that we surround ourselves with and how we feel in that space. As I began to work with children in a museum setting, I also discovered my love for teaching. I combined those passions into a career as an art teacher. It brings me immense joy to see the impact in the energy of a space when children are surrounded by the art they have created. Eventually, I shifted from museum work to teaching art and art history full-time in public middle schools.

While I continued to explore and delve into this journey, I also became aware of feng shui. It was quite clear to me that I had been tapping into an intuitive knowing of feng shui while studying art history and museum studies, and in teaching. Soon after I had this awareness, I formally embarked on my feng shui studies, and began coaching others around how their space impacts every area of their lives.

As I continue to explore and make connections in my life and work, I recall the lasting impact that one Humanities class and its amazing teacher had on my life, not only in opening doors to new worlds, but in revealing the path to who I am meant to be.

Reflection

How often do you tolerate situations because you think you have no choice?

____

____

____

____

In what ways can you embrace your passions in your daily life?

____

____

____

____

What daily practices do you engage in that can support you in shining your light even in the face of doubt, fear, or conflict?

____

____

____

____

MY DREAMS CHOSE ME

Kelly Mishell

The air grew cold. I rubbed my hands together. We'd received instructions to dress in layers, so that morning I wore a tee-shirt, sweater, down jacket, skinny jeans, and UGG boots. In a crowd of warmly-dressed people, no one would have guessed it was August in Princeton, New Jersey, until you stepped outside of the hotel ballroom.

Two weeks before my fiftieth birthday, I flew with my husband Dan from California to attend a weekend relationship retreat. Six months before, we'd worked on reviving our passionless, eggshell-laden, nine-year marriage. We shared high hopes that this intensive coaching experience would jumpstart the healing of our marital wounds.

The arctic temperature in the room was intended to facilitate our breakthroughs. I wasn't sure how being cold would help, but the chill certainly kept me alert. Since the workshop's focus was self-development, we were directed to sit away from our partners to dissuade any potential glares of, "See? I told you so!" Dan and I complied, understanding how one ill-timed look could have thwarted our desired outcome.

For weeks, I had been contemplating having a half-century in my rearview mirror. The question I kept avoiding now filled in my head. "What the heck am I doing with my life?"

When I was fifteen, I had my future mapped out with certainty. I'd be a successful working actress, be married to the love of my life by the time I was twenty-five, and have two children by the time I hit thirty. Back then, it all seemed plausible. Performing had been my passion and something that came naturally to me. Plus, I had been taught to "have a plan, then work your plan."

How wrong I was! In Hollywood, acting jobs were few and far between, regardless of how good my acting chops were. Online dating proved equally dismal.

After ten years of auditions with no boyfriend in sight, I considered I'd have more success in New York. The theater was my real love anyway. But, the closer I got to making that move, I came up with every excuse not to go. I told myself it was too cold and all the apartments were rat-infested. In truth, I felt terrified.

I'd been beaten down after years of being rejected by casting agents, being in awful relationships, and living hand-to-mouth. Although I craved the adventure, I couldn't dredge up enough faith in myself to move 3,000 miles away from my family only to fall on my face again. Self-doubt and fear of failure paralyzed me.

To assuage my disappointment, I embarked on a hometown project, planning my twenty-year high school reunion. That's where I reconnected with Dan. Our chemistry sparked immediately. I marveled that this bright, thoughtful, intelligent boy had become the man I had waited for. Life in Los Angeles began to look brighter.

We married two years later, and the births of our darling daughters followed. I thought myself rescued from a dull existence. My prince had come and given me a family. My purpose seemed clear—or so I thought.

Dan traveled for work, and I felt utterly trapped in the life I had thought would save me. I had the husband and children I'd dreamed of, yet I wanted to scream, "Why is my life *still* so unfulfilling?" My discontent permeated our lives.

On the second of the three ten-hour days at the retreat, I sat at a round table, bleary-eyed and mainlining caffeine, with six women right up front by the stage. The first day's activities included exercises where I'd intimately shared with them information I'd never revealed before, even to Dan. These women, whom I now considered friends, safely held space for my revelations.

After lunch, the ballroom lights dimmed. On the giant screen in front of us, the word REGRET flashed, catching my attention. A young African-American man spoke rhythmically, in rap style, "A study was conducted in hospitals of a hundred people nearing the end of life. They were asked to reflect on their life's biggest regret. They said they didn't regret what they'd done, but what they *didn't* do." His eyes looked out from the video. "I ask you, will your last words be, 'if only I had …'?"

Every syllable sank deep into my core. This man, or some divine entity, spoke directly to me. "People don't choose dreams; dreams choose *them*."

As the man built to a crescendo of conscience, my heart burned with regret. I had been playing small, putting my dreams on the back burner, and covering up my light. This complete stranger called me out. I felt the deep ache of being imprisoned by fear and, for the very first time, examined the future I was creating. I imagined myself old and weak, lamenting a half-lived life. "If only I had reached my God-given potential."

Despite the veil of the darkened room, I squeezed back the tears welling in my eyes. My body quivered with shame. I didn't want to confess my sin of living in paralyzing fear and self-doubt. My sobs became uncontrollable. I waited for the inevitable, "Are you okay?" No one spoke, each intent on the stranger's powerful message.

The wasted time and talent felt unforgivable. Suddenly, my sorrow became my fuel. I sat up straighter. I saw clearly that my dreams and internal fire are a divine gift! How dare I disappoint God—and myself!

Rachel, the woman sitting to my right, gently slipped her arm around my shoulders, her eyes still focused on the screen. It was like she instinctively knew my opposing needs for support and privacy. She inched closer to me as if to say, "I've got you. You're not alone."

A deep internal excavation took place, exposing a lifetime of denial. At that moment, I realized I could no longer bear the misery of hiding. I knew I needed to make a decision: I could either continue on the path of denial or I could be the courageous, powerful woman I was born to be.

It was my choice and mine alone. No one else would make it for me—not my husband, my daughters, my parents, or my friends. In that dark ballroom, I vowed that forty years down the road I would not have regrets. It was time to play a bigger game and live my purpose-driven life.

Later in our room, I shared my epiphany with Dan. He listened as I confessed that I felt many of our marriage woes centered around me blaming him for my unhappiness. I felt embarrassed by my behavior. I told him that, although I didn't know the next step, I was committed to living my passion and purpose. Just speaking those words felt like the freedom that I hadn't experienced in years.

The breakthrough for which I had traveled 3,000 miles was far from what I expected, but it changed me forever. The real Kelly was reborn on that beautiful August evening.

We arrived back in California, excited and eager, despite my true purpose remaining a mystery. I felt the Universe had a plan for me; I just needed to discover it. I trusted that, in time, I would receive my answer.

Back home, I took up meditation as a morning practice. Sitting on the living room floor, invariably with the cat in my lap, I focused intensely on what I wanted, why I wanted it, and how I wanted to feel having achieved it. Having that much clarity felt opposite of the muddled feelings I'd had before the retreat.

Two weeks later, I received an e-mail from a friend endorsing a life coaching academy. Excited and inspired by how our relationship coach changed so many lives, I considered, "Was this a hand in the darkness reaching out to me?"

The answer aligned perfectly with the essence of me. I loved listening to and helping people but hadn't considered that it was my life purpose. I envisioned utilizing my acting skills to speak on public stages, inspiring others the way I'd been inspired. Finally! The puzzle pieces fell together. No longer would I take my divine gifts for granted. I signed up for the academy.

Embracing my truth and shining my light changed my life in miraculous ways. In my fifties, I feel younger than ever and have done things I would never have expected, like starting a business. Some days still seem daunting, but I now trust my inner guidance will lead the way. My perceived failures were a gift of Divine redirection. Today, I let purpose and passion move me forward into the future.

It's my time to shine. No regrets.

Reflection

How do you think the room temperature at the retreat Kelly describes impacted the attendees, and why was this strategy important?

What childhood dreams have you given up on? What would happen if you resurrected them?

Are there relationships in your life where you've changed yourself to fit in? Why? What might happen if you were true to yourself?

FINDING MY TRUE NORTH

Tarah Abram

My alarm clock rang. I reached over, hit the snooze button, and burrowed my head in my pillow. I had no desire to get up, knowing a "same old thing" kind of day faced me. I wondered, was raising my kids going to be the biggest highlight of my life? Sure, I always wanted to be a mom, and I loved being one, but I didn't feel fulfilled or happy. My life lacked adventure.

The day-to-day tasks of running errands, cleaning, and cooking left me no quality time to spend with my kids. Most days I felt like Cinderella or a housemaid. Work, work, work, and when I finished, more work. Well, until once a year when we got a week off. Not! Heck, even vacation time turned into work time so we could get all caught up.

"Get up, Tarah, or you'll be late. Stop complaining; you have many things to be grateful for."

I rose, made my kids breakfast. After I drove them to school, I tackled laundry, cleaned up the kitchen, and focused on my to-do list. I kept the house neat and tidy just as I had when I was a kid because both my parents worked and had side businesses. It felt like everything then was up to me, and because my husband worked shift work, I continued to feel that way.

The truth was I was bored. I wondered if my existence would only amount to day-to-day drudgery. That thought weighed heavily on me. "You've survived preemie babies. Cancer. A hysterectomy. There must be more!"

During difficult times in my life, I read all kinds of books and tapped into the energy around me. These tactics always guided me to increased self-knowledge. It was time to do that again.

One morning over coffee as I tuned into my energy forecast, a compelling advertisement for an online course showed up on my screen. I watched the video. It intrigued me and set my wheels spinning. "Could this be real? It could be a scam, Tarah." I took the plunge anyway.

In my first class, the instructor asked, "Who would you bet on? I mean, really bet on—if you could go back to school, sit in a classroom, and pick one person who you thought would have done something great, who would that be?"

"Me," I thought. I sat up straighter. I knew I could count on myself to accomplish anything and make sure it was done and done right. I could control the outcome.

"Find someone doing what you want to do and ask them to mentor you," the instructor told me.

How could I find someone who did what I wanted to do? I didn't know anyone like that, so I searched the internet and found a free, basic astrology course.

Lisa, a feisty lady with a New York accent, taught the course. Her sense of humor made me feel at home right away as we had so many similar interests. After our first virtual meeting, I knew she was the one to mentor me.

Deciding to enroll in Lisa's year-long business program was the biggest "yes to me" decision I had ever made. In the past, I'd studied knowing the expected outcome. This time, I had no clue where this journey would take me and THAT sounded like an adventure, kind of like taking a random road trip and seeing where you ended up. And that was exactly what my soul sought.

What I didn't expect was the reaction of raised eyebrows when I shared what I was doing. People asked me questions I couldn't answer logically. Is this a good choice? What are you even doing? They couldn't understand that I just knew in my bones I needed this.

That summer, my kids safely settled with my parents, I set off for Florida for a two-and-a-half day training. It was my first time traveling alone, and I was meeting a stranger I'd met on the internet. That wasn't at all weird, right?

The first piece of advice Lisa shared was to find our Seventh Power, a new concept to me. The Seventh Power is a kind of family based on connection and relationship, which goes beyond a traditional family. It consists of people who are on the same journey as you, who cheer you on, and support you when the ugly crying begins.

The relationships with women from Lisa's tribe felt different from other long-time friendships I had. We were aligned because we shared a mission and a similar path. It astounded me that I could so quickly and deeply connect with women whom I had never met before. Our shared purpose and mindset made it possible.

Soon after my Florida trip, I had the opportunity to join Lisa's leadership team. I knew I could learn more, but I also built and nurtured new relationships with people I had never met in person. As we worked together—and it was work—I learned so much quickly. How different from the old days of drudgery! I didn't even mind the stress; I found it kind of fun.

The work itself didn't scare me but internal fears that I didn't even know I had bubbled up. My introverted nature balked at being seen on the internet. I felt vulnerable. To be successful, I'd have to be visible. I'd have to stand out. Even so, all I wanted to do was to safely hide behind my computer screen.

Over the next few months, it became clear who truly supported me. Some people I thought were supportive disappeared. I'm sure that I seemed crazy to some, shifting as I had from the conservative mom life I'd led to the one I was growing into. My mentor was right: I had to step outside my existing circle to discover what awaited me on the other side.

Once I stepped out of that comfort zone, people just started to show up. Other mentors came into my life. I even became an international best-selling author thanks to one mentor, Linda. She told me that when you shine your light for others, it shows them what is possible for them and lights their path.

The clearer I got with myself and resolved my worries, more people came into my life who were aligned with my journey. I met other women business owners with similar mindsets: we liked our "woo," supported each other, and we believed ourselves stronger together. While we had different businesses at various stages of growth, we shared the same vision.

Badass business ladies became friends who pushed me even further. Opportunities came my way, and it felt a little crazy to say yes to game changers I wouldn't have imagined a year before. When my fears crept in, my Seventh Power guided me back to my true north, supporting me a hundred percent of the way.

The opportunity came to travel with one of my life-long friends Lana to meet some of my Seventh Power sisters in person, and that took things to a whole new level. Meeting fantastic women from all over the globe was like meeting family members for the first time. I had never felt more supported and connected. We were a tribe with an itch to change the world, and make it a better place.

And, for that, I'll skip the snooze button and leap into action, filled with gratitude for both my families.

Reflection

Describe a time when you knew you were being called to do or participate in something.

How has working with a mentor or advisor changed the way you see yourself, your life, and your business?

Who makes up your Seventh Power Sisterhood and why?

Chapter Five

CLAIM THE SPOTLIGHT

TAKING OFF MY INVISIBILITY CLOAK

Dr. Debra L. Reble

As I opened the closet door in my office, I saw the white FedEx package sitting on top of a box, precisely where I'd placed it six months before. When the package arrived in the mail, I'd noticed the return address, and couldn't bring myself to open it. It felt like a hot potato, too painful to touch without getting burned. Not ready to deal with the cascade of emotions it would unleash, I buried the package in the closet—along with the painful memories that accompanied it.

Several months before this package arrived, my former mentor Bob sent me an e-mail to ask if I would endorse his new book. Reading it, I felt as if the wind had been knocked out of me. In sheer disbelief, I cried, "How could he ask this of me?"

This wasn't just any book. This was a spiritual book to which I had contributed hundreds of hours. I had a hand in the curating, outlining, and writing. It represented twenty-five years of my dedicated service to my longtime friend and mentor, and to the spiritual foundation he had created. It was also a painful reminder of the years I had spent in yet another supporting role—a role I had played with just about every male relationship in my life.

Bob wasn't the first male spiritual guru I'd placed on a pedestal, but I was determined that he would be the last. And so, I offered my congratulations, but cordially declined to write an endorsement of "his" book.

Yet, as empowering as my reply felt, Bob's e-mail had triggered a deep disappointment within me—disappointment in his actions, but even more, disappointment in myself for devoting so much of my time, energy, and resources to getting his spiritual message out instead of my own.

"Why are these feelings coming up again now?" I wondered. A few years ago, I had blessed and released the relationship from my life. I thought I had healed my hurt and disappointment, and forgiven both him and myself—but apparently, some of the old feelings still lingered.

During the winter and spring of 2015, my beloved golden retriever, Cammi, was struggling with cancer. As I held sacred space for her to heal, I hoped for Bob's spiritual guidance and support. It was a difficult time for me, and I communicated that clearly—yet, I rarely heard from him. I always had to be the one to reach out. When we did talk, our conversations centered on him, his projects, and his life.

This wasn't the first time I'd felt his emotional detachment, self-involvement, and lack of empathy, but it was the first time I fully realized that my longtime friend and mentor wasn't there for me, and hadn't been for some time—maybe ever.

On May 23, 2015, my sweet fur baby passed under her favorite shade tree in our backyard, surrounded by family and friends. I desperately wanted Bob's spiritual perspective on her death, so I texted him to let him know she had passed, and eagerly awaited his phone call.

Instead, I got a text in return: "Blessings … Thanks for letting me know."

Although his indifference was another excruciating blow to my already-broken heart, the Divine knew that I needed a wake-up call to let go of the relationship and my dependence on it. That moment was the emotional catalyst that gave me the strength and courage to finally release the relationship.

However, the emotional pain which arose from deep within me when I saw that package sitting there in my closet alerted me that there was more healing to be done. Whatever was hiding underneath needed to come into the light. It was time to have a sacred chat with my vulnerability.

Ensconced in the safe sanctuary of my burgundy leather chair in my office, I leaned into the pain that threatened to engulf me. As I closed my eyes, a flurry of feelings whirled around me like a cyclone. I was flooded with thoughts like, "Why am I here again?"

I took some deep, intentional cleansing breaths, a signal to my brain to step aside and let my heart lead the way. I touched the center of my chest, put my attention there, and dropped into my heart space. I realized I had created, in my chair, a sacred space of love where I was safe to unravel and release the pain. Here, in my heart space, I would find the solace, resolution, and transmutation of my pain into power.

I picked up my journal and started my sacred conversation. "Why am I feeling so vulnerable and deeply sensitive about the relationship?" I asked. "Why did I react so strongly to finding the book? What am I being guided to see and release here?" As I wrote the questions, I could feel my heart open and connect to my Divine source.

From deep within, I heard the whisper of spirit.

"This is not about Bob. It's about you—about your codependency pattern and how it distracts you from embracing your truth, stepping into your power, and fulfilling your dreams. It's a pattern of caretaking, putting others first (especially men), and catering to their needs before your own. This started at a young age when you had to care for your two younger brothers because your mom abandoned you. You became a surrogate parent. Even when you went to live with your dad, you continued this pattern. You took on this self-sacrificial, caretaker role with your father, brothers, boyfriends, husbands, and spiritual teachers ... every male relationship you've ever had—except for your current husband. You broke the pattern with him."

In all of those relationships, I had elevated others' wants, desires, and needs above my own. If they wanted something, I made it happen. I became invisible so they could be more visible. I stayed behind the scenes so they could be center stage. I gave away my power so they could be more powerful.

Until now, I hadn't realized my relationship with Bob had fallen into the exact same pattern. He was the spiritual teacher, and I was the student. I had outgrown the teacher a long time ago; yet, I still deferred to him as my "guru." I conceded my power to him as I had done with all the men in my life.

Even when I was given the position of co-director of his foundation, there wasn't anything collaborative or communal about it. I operated as an assistant by organizing workshops and retreats, and coordinating his individual sessions. I was his "Girl Friday" who worked behind the scenes, making sure everything went smoothly so that the foundation would thrive—and so my mentor would remain in the spotlight.

During all of this, I was content to stay in my comfort zone. I couldn't envision myself a spiritual leader, so I sat on the sidelines, hoping no one would notice me or ask for my input. I deferred to him when we co-led workshops, hesitant to share my truth, especially if it differed from his. I chose to shrink from sight, swallow my voice, and suppress my power—to remain invisible rather than face my fears of not being good enough, wise enough, or worthy enough to spiritually lead. But while this codependent pattern temporarily filled the void left by my insecurity and self-doubt, it was not aligned with what my soul wanted; it was a path of suffering.

Bowed over my journal with tears streaming down my face, I made a new choice. In that moment, I fully chose to claim sovereignty over my own life—to stop compromising myself by continuing to play small. If I wanted to live a life of authentic service and fulfill my soul's purpose as a spiritual leader, I had to affirm I was strong, capable, and worthwhile, and that I didn't need anyone's validation or permission to express myself. That, in turn, meant changing the patterns of how I operated in my relationships—even those relationships I thought were behind me.

I got up from my chair and went to the closet. As I cut the tape on the package I'd been avoiding for six months, I felt the final layer of pain peel away. Taking a deep breath, I opened my heart, and opened the book.

I slowly flipped through the book, recognizing many instances of my work throughout. When I came to the gratitudes page, I paused. As I suspected, I found my name listed along with the many clients, sponsors, and friends who had a hand in creating the book. Nowhere did it mention the major part I had played in its creation—yet, now, I felt no charge around this revelation. I was spiritually complete with this lesson.

In my contemplation, I almost bypassed the handwritten inscription in the front of the book. It spoke lovingly of our friendship and the soul connection we shared. In gratitude, I blessed the soul purpose for which Bob and I came together, and released the rest.

Letting go of my codependent patterns in my relationships did more than take me outside my comfort zone; it transformed me in ways I never thought possible. I began to put my time, energies, and resources into my own spiritual work. I followed my heart, took a leap of trust, and said, "Yes!" to stepping out onto my own stage.

With the assistance of my friend and publisher Linda Joy, I gradually started putting myself and my message out into the world while at the same time embracing and letting go of my fear of visibility. I shifted my traditional psychology practice to one more aligned with my more intuitive and spiritual gifts. I began writing my own weekly blog, recorded a successful podcast series, and became an expert columnist for Aspire magazine. In May 2016, my book *Being Love* became an international best seller.

Today, I'm taking another step outside my comfort zone by launching my first webinar and on-line course. This is stretching me to show up fully as an expert in my field and to say "Yes!" to the bigger purpose the Divine has in store for me.

Taking the leap of visibility wasn't easy for me as it brought up all my self-doubt and insecurity. But each time I want to shrink, play small, or stay in my comfort zone, I focus on my soul's purpose: to be a lightworker at a time when our world needs me. I choose to shine my light because when I shine, others can see their reflection, take a step forward, and light the path for those behind them.

Breaking free of my past patterns brought me into my authentic truth. It is the light of my being that must shine forth beyond everything—for that is my connection to my Divine source, my full self-expression in life. I dare to be seen, heard, and acknowledged as the Divine essence I am. I choose to shine brightly, sparkle brilliantly, and shimmer radiantly so that you can feel the light shining brightly in your own heart, and beam it out for all to see. When you do, may the gracious being of your soul shine through, and manifest as love into the world.

Reflection

Do you have a pattern that shows up repeatedly in your relationships? What is this pattern? Does it serve you?

Is there a relationship in your life that's over but is still causing you pain? How can you lean into your vulnerability, release it, and grow from the experience?

Where in your life are you giving away your power so others can feel more powerful?

EMERGING

Kris Groth

Three weeks in a row, I listened to a live workshop over the phone. In each session, the instructor asked us to post questions or share with the group. I desperately wanted to join in, but my heart raced, my chest tightened with a dense ball of anxiety, as my finger hovered over the button that would connect me with the group. I just couldn't get myself to join in. The battle within me raged between the desire to be seen and heard versus the fear of being seen and heard.

Images floated through my mind of times when I tried to share my thoughts and was ignored, teased, or misunderstood. I retreated to my inner sanctum where I could feel safe, knowing my words failed me once again.

After the last call ended, I sat in silence with tears welling up in my eyes. There may be safety in hiding, but there was no fulfillment or joy. I didn't want to live my life like that and set that example for my kids. The time had come to take a chance and come out of hiding. I had to overcome that fear and share my gifts with the world.

Sometime later, the most powerful and vivid vision came to me: I would write a book as a way to bring healing to more people. The message was so intense that I couldn't dismiss it. It stayed with me, even though I pushed it aside for over six months. Writing a book couldn't possibly be something I was meant to do. Could it?

I fought against accepting that vision. It must be a mistake. But, somewhere deep within me, I knew the truth. I was a writer and this knowledge clashed with my long-held beliefs: I wasn't good enough, nobody wanted to hear what I had to say, and words were not my friends.

Ideas came in a flurry, and suddenly I knew what my book would be about. Never mind that I had no idea how to write a book. As luck would have it, the next day I received information about an online book-writing course. My soul pushed me to go beyond what I believed I could, presenting opportunities and help just when I needed them.

That urge to write wouldn't go away and kept nudging me onward. The message I heard was, "You are more than you have become." I saw how much I had limited myself and shut down. In my pattern of hiding and protecting myself, I confined myself to a tiny box. Now my soul was pushing me to emerge and be more. I was scared to death. What if I couldn't do it? What if I failed? What would others think?

My soul and angels provided inspiration and encouragement. You can do this.

A knowing that I wasn't alone and had help filled me with new confidence. I referred to them as "my Divine writing team" and connected with the angels whenever I sat down to write or when I needed a boost. I felt them wrap me in a warm blanket of loving support. I began to believe that I could write a book.

Every day as I sat down to write, I connected with my team. Words flowed through me as if from somewhere else. I let go and just allowed them to come. My writing felt easy, effortless. Beyond that, I felt lit up from the inside. I felt excited about writing a book. Each day became an adventure as I had no idea where the story would go;

it was revealed to me as I typed. The Divine moved through me, and my role was that of a vessel through which the story came into form to be shared with the world.

I wrote the first draft in less than six months, just as my vision had predicted. I felt proud of that accomplishment. Despite my excitement, I kept secret the fact that I had a draft book written, telling only a couple of people closest to me.

What kept me from sharing and celebrating this considerable accomplishment and all the joy that came with it? Fear. Fear of judgment. Fear of what others would think of me and my book. Fear of failure. What if I wasn't good enough? What if my book stank? My greatest fear of all was of truly being seen.

I'd poured my heart and soul into that book. Even though it was fiction, it contained a glimpse of the real me, my core and my essence, which I rarely shared with anyone. The fear of baring my soul and allowing it to be vulnerable to criticism, judgment, or attack, felt like standing naked in front of the crowd with my invisibility cloak removed. If I kept that book to myself, nobody would even know that I had written it. I would be safe.

My soul, along with my angels, pushed me yet again. Whenever I found myself in a well of self-doubt, they sent me new ideas and motivation to keep going. I felt the urgency and importance of sharing my message, and the healing light and energy it contained. The world needed my book. I couldn't give up!

Each step in the process brought another level of fear to the surface, giving me an opportunity to acknowledge and heal it. Just when one level got cleared, another layer came up and knocked me on my butt. It felt like I took one step forward and two steps back.

Editing brought out my perfectionism, and, along with it, fears of being judged, criticized, and found lacking. I journaled through it all and realized my book might never be perfect, but neither was I. The Divine had chosen to bring this story through me for a reason, and it wasn't because I was perfect. My role was sharing wisdom with those who needed it in a form they could relate to. My story would be accepted for what it held and brought to others regardless of its flaws.

By the time I submitted my final draft, I felt satisfied with how the book turned out. But once again, fear tried to put me back in my prison, keeping my voice hidden and dulling my light.

My finger lingered over the submit button for at least five minutes. How hard could it be to push one little button? I had been working toward this moment for almost a year. My hand shook as it hovered over the "enter" key; my body trembled with muscles clenched and tense. I could hardly breathe.

Enough! I grew tired of being afraid. I'd outgrown the box of old expectations that had kept me hidden and small. No longer could I ignore my gifts. I had so much more to offer, more to give.

I took a moment to create a sacred space to connect with my soul and my angels, just like I had done when I was writing. I lit a candle and said a little prayer, asking my Divine writing team to gather round. I wrote the book with loving, nurturing energy, and wanted to submit it in the same environment. As I envisioned my team surrounding me and my book, my body relaxed. A wave of peace flowed through me. My mind calmed and quieted.

I asked, "Is this book complete?" In my mind's eye, I saw light shining out from between its covers, radiating like the sun, glowing and expanding. I felt myself glowing as well. My soul shone brightly, without restriction or limitation. I felt free, boundless, and expansive. I had been given the gift of birthing a book and filling it with light. It was time to let that light out into the world to illuminate the path for others. This vision and all the support around me gave me the confidence I needed.

At that moment, I understood that my insecurities were insignificant compared to the positive impact my book could create. I had to let go of my book and allow it to soar. My finger pushed the button to submit the manuscript to my publisher. My angels supported me to finish what I started. I released a deep breath I hadn't realized I was holding. I had done it!

I wish I could say that all of my fears and insecurities disappeared as soon as I submitted my manuscript but I can't. Each step closer to publication raised new worries, but I didn't let them derail me. I used fear as a cue for me to go deeper into myself, and take the opportunity to release and heal old baggage. With each examination, my soul's windows got clearer, allowing my light to shine brighter. And that is what my soul wants most—to *shine*!

Reflection

What have you avoided doing because you played small and crammed yourself into a proverbial box?

____

____

____

____

Who is on your Divine team and how do they support you?

____

____

____

____

Have you ever achieved something powerful (like completing the first draft of your book) but didn't stop to recognize your achievement and celebrate? Why do you think you avoided celebrating?

____

____

____

____

BROKERING A NEW FUTURE

Ann Sanfelippo

If you talk to anyone with an amazing success story, I'm certain that they will be able to pinpoint for you at least a few times in their lives when they had a choice: to stand their ground and shine their light, or to hide away in the darkness.

I'm no different. I've been blessed to be enormously successful in my life—but I didn't start off with the confidence, mindset, and entrepreneurial superpowers I have now. In fact, I started with pretty much nothing—a negative bank balance, a life that had just imploded after a divorce, and zero faith in myself and my ability to create the kind of life I wanted. I was literally hiding in my parents' back bedroom. I wasn't just refusing to shine, I was refusing to even leave the house! I've shared this story elsewhere, so I won't rehash it here; let's just say that I got myself over that hump by opening my mind enough to receive the biggest gift imaginable to me at the time: a path to wealth and self-reliance created through real estate investments.

At many points along my path, I've been presented with the choice to hide or to shine. In fact, that choice is before me again, right now. Because of the success I created through real estate investing, I was asked to speak for a company that trains individuals in investment strategies. For the past decade, I've been traveling the world, teaching others how to build wealth and create financial security for themselves. Along with speaking, I've also been growing my own real estate portfolio, as well as perfecting my personal formula for entrepreneurs to follow to attract and build wealth through my Wealth Attraction Academy™.

My life is amazing, and very full. But the time has come to step up again, and create something even bigger.

You see, although I've been enormously successful as a speaker/trainer, I recently realized something profound: Financial success, visibility, and influence do not necessarily equal fulfillment. Despite the fact that I've taken the stage in front of tens of thousands of people over the past decade, I have been dimming my light. I haven't been following *my* dreams, because I've been too busy working toward someone else's.

One day, I woke up and realized I'd become something I never thought I'd be again: someone's employee.

Not that there's anything wrong with working for someone else—there's not, for many. It's just not for me. Although my situation with the company is that of an independent contractor, I found myself allowing someone else to control my time and set what I was worth. I was losing my life balance again. I found myself expending more energy on someone else's mission than on my own. Whenever this happens, I know that there is something fundamentally out of balance. I can't operate as a creator in my life if I'm too busy to think about my own goals and dreams, let alone take action on them.

This process of reevaluation isn't new. In fact, it started in earnest a couple of years ago after a conversation with a friend who said "Ann, why are you choosing to play small? You deserve to *shine*."

I thought about those words deeply that night, and for many nights and days afterward. What did it mean, to "shine," I wondered?

Was I really standing on the sidelines and playing small, as it had been implied? What would my life look like if I decided to shine for real?

I didn't know, but I decided it was time to find out.

Less than a year later, my Wealth Attraction Academy was born. This model is my vehicle to help purpose-driven entrepreneurs manifest the lives of their dreams. It's a big piece of the light I want to bring into this world. I don't want to be the only star on the stage—I want others to shine just as brightly as I do, so we can all be brighter together!

Another piece of what I'm creating is a real estate brokerage. This isn't under the umbrella of the company for whom I train, but my own creation. Thanks to my twenty-five years in real estate, I know that if I want to empower others to create greater wealth, I need to reach as many entrepreneurs and investors as possible, while at the same time empowering real estate agents to maximize their potential. In my brokerage, agents will get more leads, close more deals, and make more money with less effort—all while helping their clients become wealthy, too! This way, everyone works smarter, not harder.

To me, the capacity to shine in our lives comes down to our self-definitions. When I first stepped onto this path, I was mourning the loss of my identity as a wife and partner. I had to let those old definitions go in order to redefine myself as a speaker, trainer, entrepreneur, and real estate mogul. Now, I'm moving once again through that tight, uncomfortable place where I'm rewriting my own story and making some crucial decisions—not about who I am, but about who I want to become.

Do I want to be a person who stays in her comfort zone, or someone who pushes her own boundaries? Do I want to be a person who plays just small enough to avoid claiming the full spotlight, or do I want to be someone who chooses to shine in her life no matter what—even when it seems scary, awkward, or borderline crazy?

When we make the choice to shine in our lives, it often means giving up some of the self-definitions we hold dear. We can no longer put our own mission and purpose on the back burner, just because to keep our status quo in place. Sometimes, shining our light means changing a relationship or your work status, as I'm doing. But more often, it simply means seeing yourself in a new light—the light of your own awesome possibility.

We are all reinventing ourselves in one way or another. Remember, change always seems awkward before it becomes elegant! My wish for you is that, in the midst of all of your transitions, you find the most amazing definition of you—and that, when you step onto your own stage, you shine with all your might.

Reflection

Just because you're successful doesn't mean you're shining in your greatness. Where in your life have you achieved success but still been playing small?

How can you leverage your genius to create something original and needed in the world?

How are you reinventing yourself right now? How can you give yourself the space to "try on" this new you?

Chapter Six

EMBRACE YOUR EMPOWERMENT

BEYOND BRAVE: A LOVE STORY

Michele Greer

By the time I'd received that last beating, I'd endured various forms of domestic abuse for over three-and-a-half years. It felt like a lifetime. The state filed charges against my abuser based upon input from the emergency room and investigating officer.

Seven months later, I was called to testify against the man I thought loved me. Being in the courtroom and seeing him multiple times during an extended trial brought up all kinds of feelings for me, including anger and disgust at having supported him financially and emotionally, to the detriment of all my other relationships. He hadn't even cared if I lived or died that night.

The jury convicted him, and the judge sentenced him to more than four years in prison. Meanwhile, I struggled to heal both my broken body and my broken spirit. I felt as though I was trapped in a dark pit, trying to claw my way out—just as I'd felt in that relationship.

Each day felt like a blur, and I didn't know if I would make it to the next. I didn't know if I even wanted to. I felt disconnected from my body, numb, and profoundly broken.

I asked myself, "Why did this happen to me? How could I have been so naive and vulnerable to believe him? Why had I stayed so long with someone who abused me?"

A miracle had saved me from that relationship, and I didn't believe I could survive that pain again. I slid a mask over my face, built a wall around my heart, and swore that no one would ever hurt me again.

I clung to "my story," and my story became my reality. I couldn't let it go. I desperately wanted people to understand that ending that relationship felt like a death. That night, I lost the person I had loved. That night was the last time we spoke. I packed up and moved all of his and his children's belongings out of my house.

I hated being home because my house had been a crime scene. I felt ashamed and judged by everyone. Well-meaning people would comment on how lucky I was to be alive, and that I was so much better off without him. At that time, I didn't believe it.

I desperately wanted for someone to say "I get it" or "I understand." No one spoke those words. That hurt. I felt isolated and alone. My therapists validated my feelings. Unfortunately, their validation kept me in my victim mentality.

I obsessed with being thin, my way of exercising control and power. I numbed out by drinking too much and frequently went out. I ate foods that were bad for me and listened to music that made me cry. I wondered what might have been…if only he had been different.

I wore a mask of perfection. I plastered a smile on my perfectly made-up face, dressed in the latest fashions, and wore my hair beautifully styled. My career picked up speed, and people sought me out for advice or cheering up. I was the life of every social event.

Ironically, I had acted the same way in the relationship with my abuser. I became a makeup expert to cover my bruises. I lied to family, friends, and physicians about what caused my injuries. I protected him and pretended everything was okay. Keeping my mask in place exhausted me.

My façade worked—it kept people a safe distance away. I didn't feel close to anyone. People commented about my strength. Being strong became my "new story," and I thought I was reclaiming my self-confidence and self-worth. To move past the pain, I kept myself busy, and in control, so I didn't have to do the deep work of healing my wounds.

Ten years later, I stumbled upon a YouTube video with Tony Robbins. I watched it multiple times because something about him resonated with me. The fates aligned to present me with an opportunity to attend one of his seminars. I knew something higher had led me to that video. I believed I could overcome significant life obstacles by attending Tony's event. I surrendered to that belief.

Traveling alone without even a friend to accompany me was far outside my comfort zone. Over 7,000 people attended the event, and the room's energy was palpable. Something significant called me to be raw and vulnerable. Leaning in, I surprisingly felt more comfortable than I had ever been before. I showed up and wanted to wake up because I felt like this was my only hope. The grace of God, Spirit, and the Universe were with me.

I experienced a breakthrough at the event. I felt safe. In my heart, I knew that I was around people who would not judge me. I saw and felt an incredible amount of love, grace, and compassion.

I broke wide open and showed my vulnerability. I removed my mask. I spoke my authentic truth and told my story. For the first time, I didn't mind admitting that I felt unworthy, insecure, lonely, sad, and stuck in "my story." The little girl I'd lost along the way—a child full of innocence, love, and trust—protected me like an angel. I felt so connected at a soul level after opening up and being real.

The amazing people surrounding me gave me hope. They created a safe place so I could release all that pain trapped inside me. I finally received the validation I had been longing for. They understood my loss and my pain. They understood me.

I experienced a massive shift as I unleashed my emotions. I cried again after having shut down for years. Crying felt like a tremendous release.

The biggest lesson I learned from the event is that people are more alike than they are different. When I removed my mask, showing my authentic self, I finally felt the connection I had been longing for my entire life. My courage enabled others to remove their masks and share their truths. I learned that people don't want to see someone who appears perfect on the outside. By being authentic and real, I connected deeply with other people and felt gratitude and love surrounding me.

Tony Robbins says, "If we can realize that life is always happening for us, not to us—game over, all of the pain and suffering disappears."

I embraced this quote, and it has transformed the way I look at life, and situations that have occurred. I changed my primary question when experiencing a difficult situation. I used to ask myself, "Why is this happening to me?" I now ask, "What is the gift in this? What am I supposed to learn?"

I wouldn't be the person I am today, and I wouldn't care as deeply as I do if I hadn't suffered the way I did. My worst nightmare turned out to be my greatest gift. My story would have been tragic if I didn't make the abuse and its aftermath mean something.

I learned that being strong is being vulnerable. I learned to open up and be seen by other people. Most importantly, I learned to be vulnerable with myself. I learned to ask for help, to take down the walls, and to let go of the need for perfection.

This life-changing transformation has been one of the hardest and most beautiful experiences of my life. Choosing to be conscious and wake up brought long-buried emotions to the surface, forcing me to deal with deeply-held beliefs.

In my long journey to wholeness, I finally met the love of my life. I fell in love with the one person I know is authentic, someone I can trust, someone who would never leave me, never hurt me, will always have my back, and will cherish me. That person is me. I'm forever grateful.

Reflection

Michele found true healing when she went inside and connected with her authentic self. Is this something you've experienced?

Do you see yourself still stuck in your story? What is an internal action you can choose to feel your emotions and open up?

Michele talks about the power of changing her primary question. What has been your go-to question by default? What can your new empowering question be?

KEEP SHINING BRIGHTLY

Kelley Grimes, MSW

Shortly after I started dating my husband, Tony, he left me a note on an index card that read, "Keep shining brightly." I felt surprised that not only did he recognize my light, he celebrated it. Mostly, I was amazed at how much I had grown, that I could choose someone who would.

Growing up as the youngest child, I often did not feel heard. Over time, I began to equate not being heard with not being important, and a sense of unworthiness began to take root. I found myself wanting to please others, often looking to them to acknowledge my value and worth.

My first "real" boyfriend was a charming, handsome boy from a private high school in town who knew all the right things to say—and I fell for all of them—hook, line, and sinker. He was very attentive, called all the time, and told me he loved me after a few months of dating. It was a dream come true to be with someone who appeared to value me so much.

I am not sure how long this honeymoon phase lasted because I was in denial about his controlling and abusive behavior. When he started to demonstrate jealousy, I believed he just loved me so much that he did not want anyone else talking to me. When he wanted to know exactly where I was at all times, I felt flattered that he was so interested. When he would get angry at things I did and call me names, I thought it was my fault.

When he started being physically and sexually abusive, I blamed myself. I thought if he loved me so much and yet still treated me this way, then there must be something wrong with me. Since my sense of unworthiness stuck to me like Velcro, I honestly never considered that he was the problem; instead, I tried to be a better girlfriend.

I felt so much shame and responsibility for his abusive behavior that I felt sick to my stomach most of the time. It got to the point where I could barely eat. My mother took me to the doctor, who diagnosed me with an ulcer at age sixteen. I remember the doctor asking if there was anything stressful in my life. I lied, saying everything was fine. I was too embarrassed to tell the doctor or my parents what was really going on, and the few friends who were aware of my situation didn't know how to help.

I felt lost, hopeless, and terrified of making a mistake that would lead to more abuse. Over time, I completely lost my voice, confidence, and belief in myself. I intentionally turned my light way down so as to not attract any attention from others for fear it would trigger his jealousy.

I'm not sure what would have happened if his friends hadn't stepped in. They told him that if he didn't stop abusing me they would tell me about the other girls he was dating. When they did share all of this with me, I was so relieved to stop living this lie and pretending that everything was okay. Finally, I summoned the courage to break up with him—but the real healing did not begin until shortly after the breakup.

While at a friend's party, I was called outside to find him kicking and keying my mother's car in front of a crowd of people. To my amazement, I found myself saying, "You can hurt me all you want but you cannot hurt my mother's new car!"

Actually hearing myself say that my mother's car was more valuable than I was caused an earthquake throughout my being and became a profound turning point in my life. I realized at that moment that I had to heal this deep sense of unworthiness that I carried around. I finally began to allow myself to accept the abusive things said and done to me. I vowed to take back my power and found myself setting boundaries in ways I had never done before. This empowering insight forever changed my perception of myself as well as how I expected to be treated by others.

A few years later, I went off to college, where I enrolled in women's studies classes and started volunteering at the Boulder County Safe House. I worked on the crisis line and in the shelter, supported women through the court process, and eventually provided domestic violence prevention trainings in schools and the community. In the process of volunteering and being there for women who were reaching out, sometimes for the first time, I heard stories that sounded very similar to mine. I witnessed tremendous courage, strength, resilience, resourcefulness, gratitude, and grace that inspired and humbled me.

I healed more from these experiences than I could ever have received from just going to counseling. I was able to recognize that I was not alone and, just like these women, I did not deserve to be treated disrespectfully. It was a powerful reminder for me to say to others what I most needed to hear—that they had value, that they were worthy, and that they were courageous to have survived so many traumas. And, my volunteering offered another gift: a deep sense of purpose that grew my confidence and belief in myself again.

After I graduated from college, I continued to fuel my passion for empowering women by volunteering for the Rape Crisis Team where I answered the hotline, supported women through the hospital process, and supervised other volunteers. When I met my husband, I had just started the training and was surprised that he was interested in what I was learning.

My healing and growth continued during my Masters of Social Work program, where I facilitated domestic violence perpetrator groups during one of my internships. Looking back, I am amazed that just ten years after leaving my abusive relationship, I was empowered enough to work with abusers and feel a depth of compassion for them that allowed me to heal even more. Through each empowering experience my light began to shine more and more brightly, and I felt compelled to pay it forward.

Healing from this abusive experience has informed everything I have done in my career, and inspired my life's purpose to empower women to speak their truth and shine their lights brightly in the world. I have learned that to shine with my whole self means not rejecting the parts of myself that are not as bright, but instead choosing to bring more love, compassion, and light to them in order to transform any residue of shame and unworthiness.

I believe this is a lifelong transformation that requires daily self-nurturing practices to reinforce the value I hold for myself as well as my continued commitment to share my experiences with others. I have seen that the more I own and express my value and worth in the world, the more brightly I shine, giving others permission to do the same.

Over thirty years later, I am blessed to work with amazing, courageous, and inspiring women every day through the non-profit Leap to Success, where our mission is to educate and empower women rebuilding their lives from domestic violence, homelessness, and other major life challenges. I believe in the power of women's stories to give hope, strength, and encouragement to others. To this day, I continue to witness the most amazing transformations as women reclaim their voices, speak their truth, and shine.

I wish I could have told my sixteen-year-old self how important she was, and that no one had the right to treat her disrespectfully in any way. I wish I could have reminded her that she was smart, creative, kind, resourceful, resilient, and courageous. I wish I could have convinced her that there was nothing wrong with her, and that she was deeply loved and lovable. But the blessing is that, today, she knows all this is true, and she reminds me daily to keep shining brightly!

Reflection

Have you ever felt valueless in your life? How did that affect your choices?

How have your traumas influenced your life trajectory? What lessons did you learn from them, and how do they empower you today?

Kelley found healing in supporting other survivors of violence. Have you found healing through service? If not, how could you create this experience?

LOST AND FOUND

Jessica Dugas

I was never a fan of elevators. Looking back, I recognize it was because being in that enclosed space forced me to get up close and personal with myself. Let me tell ya, that's a lousy place to be when you don't like yourself very much. This elevator and I, however, soon became good friends because it took me to what I thought was a goodbye.

A week before I became intimately acquainted with that elevator, I received a phone call.

"Grampy's not doing well. They don't know how much time he has left," my mother said, her voice distant. With my brother, Adam, also in the ICU due to complications from metastatic melanoma, it wasn't a question of if we would visit, but when. It was time.

My husband and then-four children made the twenty-hour drive from Alabama to Connecticut. We barely made it out of Alabama before my phone rang. Grampy had passed away. Intense grief hit me that I hadn't made it home in time to say goodbye to the man—my grandfather and godfather—who helped to raise me and so greatly influenced my life.

When we arrived in Connecticut, exhausted from the drive, I melted into one of my Grammy's warm and comforting hugs. I could feel her pain and exhaustion, yet as was typical of her, there was peace. I welcomed that energy from her because there was so little of it inside me.

In due course, we made the short drive to the hospital to see Adam. On the way, we debated about whether or not we ought to tell him about Grampy. Knowing Adam's passionate personality, if he found out I hadn't told him about our grandfather, we would have had the sibling squabble of the ages!

I don't think I could have prepared myself for seeing my brother, four years younger than me, intubated and strapped to a bed. My heart hurt. I will never forget the look on his face when he saw me. He knew I was there for a reason.

After sitting with him for a moment, I summoned my courage and spoke softly, "We came because Grampy passed."

Adam just turned his head away and looked out the window.

I told him about the funeral arrangements. "At least we'll be able to visit with you while we're here," I said.

Soon, Adam grew restless and appeared uncomfortable. We made the difficult decision to leave him.

The next day, we fought the hospital rules, hoping my young children could visit with their uncle. He had lived with us for a short time, so three of my kids knew him. My youngest daughter had been born only three months earlier on the eve of his emergency brain surgery.

Overnight, Adam's condition had worsened. I watched this young man, once full of smart-ass vigor and no fear, reach out to hold my baby girl, completely forgetting all about his straps and tubes. Frustrated and exhausted by the attempt, he gave up without taking her. At that moment, I thought about all the times in my life I wished for an ounce of his fearlessness and strength. Now I just wanted to give him all of mine.

Another restless night came and went. The phone rang. No good news ever arrives in the wee hours. Adam's numbers were off. My mother wouldn't be going to the funeral.

I felt conflicted. I wanted to go to my Grampy's service, but I also wanted to be with my brother. Honestly, at that moment, I don't know what I wanted. I chose to honor my grandfather.

Grampy's funeral was a beautiful tribute to his life as was the start of his reception held at the golf course near his home. As we sat down at the club, my phone rang. Chills raced up and down my body. We needed to get to the hospital.

My husband drove, and all I could think of was that the car couldn't go fast enough. Why couldn't I teleport to his side? After what felt like years, I raced to that elevator. I had no time to think about my dislike of it, or the "me" inside it. I felt panicky. I just had to get to Adam.

When the elevator beeped on the ICU floor, I didn't want to get out. An outside force pushed me along. I felt as though I moved in slow motion to get to Adam's room. As I reached the door, I knew he was gone.

The room was dark. Quiet. Faces blurred—of mom, Adam's fiancée Cheryl, and her mother—as I rushed to my brother. His hands, resting at his side, still held warmth, symbolic of the fact that his energy lingered in the room although his human body no longer worked.

The air felt thick, and suddenly a feeling hit me, taking my breath away. Have you ever tried to breathe while the wind blows in your face? That's the feeling I had, an overwhelming sense of simultaneously releasing and receiving. I fell into a chair, hit by a realization.

My brother was gone, but in essence, so was I. I had lost myself completely over the years. A failed, abusive marriage. Not taking care of myself. Lousy health. An eating disorder. I hadn't loved myself enough to change anything, or even care that my life was a mess. Then, not knowing how to fix any of it and afraid to be anything other than what I thought others wanted me to be, I slapped on the face of newfound love and mom of the year on top of it.

Guilt washed over me. Why wasn't I thinking of Adam at that moment? Jessica, you're so selfish. But I WAS thinking about him.

Adam was there, yelling at me in the way only he could. Get your shit together. *Love* yourself. Take care of yourself. *Be* yourself. Accept nothing less than that from others.

Then jealousy reared its head. Adam had done what he wanted and was unapologetically himself. What I would have given for the tiniest bit of his bravery and power.

That elevator I feared took me to say goodbye, but it also brought me to hello—to myself. I left Adam's room that evening on a new path. To where? I could have never imagined. I spent time, in the beginning, paving the way with guilt and regret for not loving myself sooner. Losing two influential people in my life so close together kept me numb. When that numbness wore off, I realized I didn't truly love myself either.

Sometime later, Adam visited me in a dream. He and I walked in the cemetery where he was buried, and we sat together by his grave. We laughed, bickered, and laughed some more like we always had.

He told me to let it all go. He said none of the nastiness I felt toward myself helped at all. "How the hell are you supposed to do your job here when you're so angry at yourself all the time?"

Job? I thought. I'm just a mom.

"You can't see it now, but just wait," he said. He then gave me a message to pass on to his fiancée, Cheryl, which I did.

I returned to my new path, now paved with love and joy. Every moment of my life continues to be an opportunity to learn and grow.

As for elevators? Bring them on! I'm not afraid to get up close and personal with myself anymore. I don't fear where I'll be when the elevator beeps, and the door opens. Over the last eight years,

I've inched closer to the woman I was meant to be, thanks to help from my angel with yellow wings, Adam. I am not the picture of perfection, and for the first time, I don't want to be. I want to be me: a beautiful, messy, work in progress. I choose to live with joy every single day. I decided to share my gifts and talents with the world without fear.

I love me.

Reflection

How has the loss of someone you love caused you to reflect on your life? What changes did you make as a result?

What is something you can do for yourself today to honor where you are on your journey?

What's one way you can choose today to live more authentically—to be you, even if you're a "beautiful, messy work in progress"?

Chapter Seven

BELIEVE IN MIRACLES

VALUING LIFE

Marquetta "Martini" Goodwin

They say a broken heart never killed anyone, but I beg to differ. I may not have the visible battle wounds and scars to prove it, but I was one of the lucky ones who lived to tell my tale.

I had a man in my life whom I adored. I worshipped the ground he walked on. He was well aware of my flaws. Even then, he'd tell me, "Mama, you're perfect in every way." He was the first man to love and accept me for *me*.

I never worried about anything when he was near. I felt safe and loved. So when he asked me to marry him, you'd think I would have said, "Hell, yeah!" I was given the opportunity to be with my modern day Prince Charming for the rest of my life. Why wouldn't I want that?

Of course, I wanted to run away with him to Reno, Nevada, but something in my intuition told me not to. He begged and pleaded, but I still said no.

A week after his proposal, my beloved called and confessed he had secretly been with someone else—his real soulmate—the entire time we had been together. He was in love, and we were done. "Sorry, it is what it is," he said. Then, he abruptly hung up the phone.

My heart stopped, and I felt sick. I tried to wrap my head around the fact that only a week before, he'd wanted me to elope with him.

By turning down his proposal, my inner wisdom had protected me. Instead of being grateful, I felt like I was being punished for following my intuition. To numb the pain of my heartbreak, I drank as if the only comfort to be found was at the bottom of a bottle of Cabernet. I slept around to feel some kind of loving connection.

One drunken night, I looked at myself in the mirror, and I didn't like who was staring back at me. There I was at the age of twenty-five, not married, not living in a house with a white picket fence, no kids or dog. Not only that, I hadn't lived up to my family's expectations of finishing college, and I didn't have a fulfilling career. Meanwhile, everyone around me seemed to be happily getting married, having kids, and moving up the corporate ladder.

I fell into a depression so low that I thought about committing suicide. I even planned my death. I got my affairs in order. I cleaned my apartment, paid the bills, and set money aside for my funeral.

Then I went to the cabinet where I'd squirreled away pills and swallowed them all, chasing them with a full bottle of my best Cabernet. I sat alone in my apartment, waiting. Suddenly, I asked, "Oh, God! What have I just done?" As my vision began to fade, and numbness in my body set in, I reached for a notebook and scribbled a goodbye. Then I lost consciousness.

Most people who contemplate suicide romanticize death, believing they will be free of their problems and finally have a sense of peace. That wasn't my experience. There was nothing glorious about my suicide.

In my state of unconsciousness, and in that space between dimensions, I missed my human existence. My heartbeat. The fullness in my belly of grandma's gumbo after church. Raindrops trickling down my skin. Babies crying in grocery stores. The sting of a paper cut received while opening a birthday card. The sun's warmth on my skin on a hot summer's day. Regret washed over me, and I realized I'd made the wrong decision. I had taken my one precious life for granted, and I wanted to live.

Miraculously, I regained consciousness. When I opened my eyes, I saw the sheer violet curtains swaying through the open window in my bedroom. I heard birds chirping and cars honking on the street below. I was alive.

Out of shame, I kept my suicide attempt a secret. I turned to spirituality to help heal my wounds. As I embraced a new way of being, I still couldn't shake the pain of losing my love or working in an unfulfilling job. Nothing in my world seemed to have changed for the better.

One night, I awoke with a pain in my chest, desperate for answers. Crying uncontrollably, I asked God, "What am I doing wrong? There's got to be more to life than this. I want to be somewhere where I can be happy. A place where I feel alive again. Please show me what to do."

A week later, I logged onto Facebook, and the first thing I saw was an invitation to stay in a restored monastery in Italy. As I read through the details, I knew it was exactly what I needed: a completely different environment under the Tuscan sun, experiencing a simple life by cooking with the chef, olive picking, meditating in a lavender garden, and living life in a whole new way.

I calculated the cost of $5,000 to cover my expenses. Unfortunately, when I looked at my bank account, I saw a whopping thirty-eight dollars. If I wanted to attend, I had only a month to raise the money. I smiled, knowing the Universe was challenging me to see just how much I wanted this and what I was willing to do to make it happen. There was no doubt in my mind I was going to make it happen no matter what. My life and sanity depended on it.

With hard work and a little magic, I did it. I got to Tuscany.

Waking up every morning to the sun streaming through my window and the heavenly sound of church bells ringing from a distance, I was overwhelmed with a sense of peace I hadn't felt in a long time. It was there in that little monastery in the hills of Chianti, Italy, that I was reminded of the dreams and goals I used to have but had pushed aside to meet the expectations of others. Why had I ever given them up?

My suicide attempt didn't have anything to do with the pain caused by my former boyfriend. The truth was more profound—it had everything to do with me.

While walking one of the trails on the monastery grounds, I realized that I was an unconventional woman who tried to be someone other than who she is, hoping to please other people. I wanted something different than what my family desired for me, and my depression stemmed from trying to achieve the unrealistic expectations that society places on me.

I wanted more for my life, and this time I was going to create it on *my terms*. It was time to make different choices, and that meant getting over a man who wasn't meant for me and leaving the job I hated. By going to Italy, I learned that if I truly valued my life, I needed to live it for me.

Today, I see that no matter how flawed or messed up life appears to be—after the heartbreaks, the losses, the disappointments, and life turns out to be something other than what we expected—life still goes on *if we allow it to*. That's the beauty of it. Every day we choose to live is a sacred gift that we give ourselves, a gift to experience all that life has to offer. That is what makes life worth living.

Reflection

When have you accepted others' expectations of you over your own? How did you feel when you made that compromise?

What keeps you tethered to this world when your heart feels broken?

Where do you go to heal and nurture yourself when you need time to regroup and re-evaluate? Do you have rituals that support you?

FLARES AND PRAYERS

Susan Kay Dahl

The first call came on a Friday morning in October, four days before my only daughter's baby was due. Ready or not, labor had begun. I was going to be a grandma! Suddenly, November seemed too long to wait to fly from Minneapolis to Tallahassee to meet my grandchild. I wanted to be there immediately. For the next two hours, the phone line became my umbilical connection to my grandson's birth. What a joyous occasion!

The next afternoon, I received a different call. My daughter was on her way to the emergency room with the baby.

"What! Why?" I said, feeling shocked.

"My phone is almost out of charge," my daughter said. "I don't have time to talk. Tell people to pray."

Knowing I needed something to do other than fret, I took a drive to a beautiful park overlooking the St. Croix River, which separated Wisconsin and Minnesota. While pacing and praying with my phone in hand, I calmed myself by snapping photos of the glorious sunset. The shadows and colors melted together in such incredible splendor. I was considering whether to share my pictures when an unknown number popped on my screen. I answered.

A shaky "Mom ..." was all I heard. The pause that followed stretched on. I had never heard my daughter breathe like that—not after a race, not when she was an excited little girl, not when she was hurt. She had been sobbing, and I could tell she was about to start again.

I needed to say something comforting, encouraging, but words wouldn't come. My thoughts were wrapped in a thick fog. I strained to hear my daughter's voice.

"Mom, they have to operate. Something inside the baby is either blocked or twisted. They won't know until they get inside. They warned us he might not make it," my daughter said. "If the Lord takes him, I will be thankful for the pregnancy and the birth experience and every minute of the joy I had with him."

I couldn't breathe. "Don't you talk like that. The baby's going to make it! Remember *Matthew 5:16*: 'Let your light so shine before men, that they may see your good works, and glorify your Father which is in heaven.'"

"Mom, I can't believe you just quoted that verse! I prayed it last night, like 400 times."

That was no coincidence. It was a spirit connection. In an instant of clarity, I knew I needed to be there to comfort my daughter.

But I had no one to comfort *me*. I stood alone on the bluff, looking out at the sunset in the only place I could have found the kind of peace that passes understanding. I couldn't lean on the Lord with all my heart. Some part of me needed to know why this was happening.

What do you do when you hear your first grandchild may not live? I wanted to shout out loud. I thought of my oldest son, who almost never cried. I told him when he was little, "When you are hurting, scream 'Ouch!' as loud as you can. It will make you feel better." I wished I could do the same thing to release my agony.

I looked again at my sunset photos. My spirit ached. How could such beauty coexist with such pain? I looked at a picture my daughter had taken of her husband, a first-time daddy, giving a thumbs up. On his lap lay a limp baby boy wearing a newborn hat. The image had been taken moments before the pediatrician arrived for a home visit. I recalled her words, "This morning when I posted that picture was the happiest moment of my life."

I returned to my car and crumpled up inside, sobbing inconsolably. My face grew puffy, and my nose was so stuffy that I struggled to breathe. Wiping my tears with my sleeve and sucking in deep breaths, I wrestled with my fear. NO! He is a *fighter*. I can't think that way. I will hold my grandson, and nothing is going to stop me from getting down there as soon as I get a flight. Hang on. Keep believing he is going to make it.

I held my face in my hands until the warmth and pressure made me smile. In my emotional confusion, I heard a voice say, "When there's no way out, there is a way *up*."

I looked to the heavens. I felt the warm hug of faith. "Please, Jesus. Let him live. I want to hold him. I need to know he will make it through this." I grabbed a pen and wrote myself calm. The thoughts spinning in my head spilled out into a poem in a gentle wave that captured the moment.

REST ASSURED.
Bring it. Sing it. SHINE your light.
Be the BEACON—Shining bright.
Sing the song that comes from YOU,
Hearts of LOVE will see this through.

Days of pain when you need healing
You can TRUST in what you're feeling
LOVED. And NEEDED. Blessed. SECURED.
That's HIS Promise.
REST ASSURED.

Back home, I found it difficult to sleep and kept checking my phone what seemed like every ten minutes. By two o'clock in the morning, I desperately wanted answers. So, I phoned the hospital.

The front desk nurse answered. "What's the security password, please?"

What? Are you kidding me? Breathe. Just breathe. Remember, you have faith. Good old faith, hope, and love. And the greatest of these is love. *Isaiah 43:4* reads, "You are precious in my eyes, and honored, and I love you." No matter what.

I confessed I didn't know the password, so the nurse asked me to name my daughter's hometown. When I'd answered correctly, he told me about my grandson's condition, called midgut volvulus with malrotation. He even spelled it for me before assuring me that the baby was stable. I felt gratitude and the spirit of peace.

I had faith that my grandson would pull through. I believed that all of the flares and prayers we had started were being seen, heard, and answered. Secure in my faith, I drifted off to sleep, hearing the song of my soul, "Nothing is greater than taking a minute, just to reflect on God's presence within it."

I woke up smiling. All that day, I made an effort to smile at everyone, everywhere. On the plane. In the hallway at the hospital. On the way to the bathroom. But the moment I saw my daughter, I lost it. I reminded myself, "Come on! *Find a way!*"

All of the love, pain, and compassion I felt gave energy to her war-torn, sleepless form. I hugged her as if I would never let go. It felt wonderful to hold her, even under devastating circumstances. I needed her. She needed me. At that moment, I loved her like a newborn all over again.

She finally got to take a nap knowing I was there to take over for her. I held and rocked and sang to my grandson. I had no idea what was to come. Even though his temperature rose and the nurses grew worried, I smiled. I was there. My faith stayed strong.

My grandson, now twenty months old, defied medical predictions. His gastrostomy tube, or G-tube, still delivers his food directly into his stomach. I love bearing witness to his curiosity and feel joy at being there for my daughter and her family. In fact, I'll be a grandma for the second time by the end of the year.

My faith is my light. I have a newfound resolve to be a beacon others can see. Just as Matthew said, I will *so* shine!

Reflection

What miracles of healing have you witnessed or have happened to you in your life?

___

___

___

___

How can you bring more love to a challenging situation today?

___

___

___

___

When you need to find a way to your inner calm, what comes to mind?

___

___

___

___

BACK DOOR BLESSINGS

Marcia Mariner

My mother and I left the doctor's office. The damp drizzle of the November dusk wet my face. As we crossed the busy street, my mother reached out and grabbed my hand. Her firm yet tender grip sent a message: *I am here. I love you. We've got this.*

I wanted my life to end right there, at fifteen. I felt ashamed and wanted to run away to hide from everyone and everything. Let the cars hit me, I thought, my mind reverting to a dissociative survival state similar to the shock and trauma I felt five years earlier when my seventeen-year-old brother had been killed in a tractor accident.

That night, I sat with my parents around our large kitchen table in our old farmhouse. A heavy gloom hung over us as we ate roast chicken and mashed potatoes in numbed silence. Three empty chairs sat around the table, a reminder of happier days when my older brother and sisters lived at home. Memories of happy family meals faded like an old photograph.

Had happiness ever really existed? I wondered.

When the phone rang, my mom jumped up to answer it. She told my sister the news. "Your sister's pregnant."

A week later my mom and I met Meredith, a social worker at an adoption agency located in a beautiful Victorian building. It had a stately and grand staircase.

Meredith greeted me with a handshake and smile, and I immediately felt safe in her presence. She exuded kindness and non-judgment. Her beautiful blonde hair was rolled into a bun. She had kind eyes and a soft-spoken presence. Ironically, she was about seven months pregnant.

Meredith took my history, asking question after question about my childhood and all the identifying information needed for her to help me and to provide the adoptive parents with as many facts as possible. What color were the father's eyes? What ethnic background was he?

Meredith assured me that my baby would be placed in the best of homes. She presented me a portfolio of a couple in their thirties. They'd been trying for some time to have a family and were eager to become parents. My gut reaction was that this couple could do a better job raising the baby than my parents or me. I wanted my baby to be happy, safe, wanted, and loved.

The potential parents were well-educated, professional, and had money. They lived on a farm and raised animals. I grew up on a farm, and I felt reassured thinking my baby would be living in a similar world to me. We'd be connected.

I trusted Meredith's judgment. She felt optimistic about this couple and what they could offer as adoptive parents. Adoptions were closed back then, which meant no contact between us would be allowed. Despite having my heart broken that I'd not get to see the baby, I agreed.

The day she was born, I saw my newborn daughter through the window of the hospital nursery. She slept soundly in a white bassinet, wearing a white crocheted hat on her head. Her face was red and imprinted with the shape of the forceps that had been used to help her through my narrow birth canal.

I named her Sheryl Anne. (I learned later that her name had been changed to Cheryl Lee.) That moment in the nursery I said hello, and also said goodbye. I made a silent vow to Cheryl that I would see her again one day. Standing there, I felt detached and frozen, which protected me from the excruciating pain I felt. I reminded myself that I was doing this because I loved her.

My mother gave an afghan she'd crocheted for the baby along with a necklace with a cross to the caseworker. We said our goodbyes to Cheryl at the hospital. I took with me her original baby bracelet, a memory of her first moments.

About a month after my baby was born, I signed the final adoption papers with Meredith and my mother as witnesses. I felt confident in my decision, which gave me the strength to go through with the process with unwavering certainty.

My parents' unconditional love during the entire process was heaven sent. I felt connected to both of them, and I always knew I was deeply loved. Their kindness and non-judgmental support of me to get through Cheryl's birth and adoption was etched in my heart.

Meredith's support also gave me a priceless gift. It opened me up to a new career path, one that had never occurred to me. After experiencing her masterful way of guiding me through a traumatic time, I knew that I was meant to pursue a career in the helping professions. I wanted to make an impact on women's lives like Meredith had made on mine.

Three years after finishing my graduate studies in psychology, I met Mark, my twin flame and now husband of almost thirty years. After that meeting, my journey to deeper purpose and prosperity quickly accelerated. Eventually, we launched our private practice and a center for wellness and personal development.

Early on in our marriage, I joined a birth parent support group. Through this group, I reclaimed my voice, my value, and my worth by healing the emptiness that was in my heart. With their support and my husband's superb research skills, I began my search to reconnect with Cheryl.

Eighteen years later, Cheryl and I met again in Florida on a ninety-degree day. She had just graduated from high school. My husband, Cheryl, her adoptive parents, and I enjoyed a lovely dinner together. Afterward, we went back to my hotel room where Cheryl shared photo albums from her childhood. I loved seeing her grow up as we flipped the pages. It all felt surreal.

We ended the evening with a walk on the boardwalk. Cheryl told me that she was not quite ready to have a relationship with me. I felt grateful for her honesty and empathy for what she might be experiencing. Respecting her boundaries was essential to me. I loved her with no expectations but wanted her to know I was always there and thinking about her.

Over the years that followed, I sent gifts for her birthday and Christmas with few responses. To have so little contact with her was excruciating at times, but I trusted that something would eventually unfold for us when she had matured more.

Six years later, Cheryl was ready. By then, she had just had her first baby and was engaged to be married. She flew up to Massachusetts with her newborn son and her adoptive mother. She met my side of her birth family.

I remember the day I felt as if we had come full circle. Cheryl invited me, my husband, and our two children, then two and five, to her wedding. After the ceremony, Cheryl's adoptive mother hugged me and thanked me for letting her raise Cheryl. I thanked her for being a loving adoptive mother, giving Cheryl all I couldn't.

I am forever grateful for my parents who embodied unconditional love in my hour of darkness. I am forever grateful to Meredith, who counseled me through that crisis. I am forever grateful to my spiritual mentors who led me to reconnect with my heart and helped me get past the pain. I am forever grateful for the birth parent support group. The "mother bears" in that group empowered me to search for Cheryl and supported me every step of the way. And I am forever grateful for my husband, who held my heart and helped me to heal so I could become the woman I am today. And, of course, I am forever grateful that I was blessed with my son and daughter, which helped me come full circle and experience the joys of motherhood.

I am forever grateful that through this "back door," my path to purpose and prosperity was revealed to me. What a blessing.

Reflection

What have you experienced in your life that, at the time, felt like the end of the world only to become a "back door blessing"?

Who has supported you unconditionally and without judgment, and how did their love make a difference to you?

How has loss shaped you, and in what ways does it still show up?

EDITOR'S NOTE

Bryna Haynes

In my world of high-powered conscious female entrepreneurs, empowerment is something that comes with the territory. "Purpose" and "service" are synonymous with "business." "Inspired action" is both part of the normal vocabulary and at the top of the daily to-do list. And "success" means living on your terms, regardless of what everyone else is saying or doing.

It's an amazing place to be, and there's no other community on earth I'd rather hang out with. The mind games and petty dramas that plague other people just don't seem to stick to us.

But what happens when you're surrounded by an incredible community of inspired women whom you love (and who reciprocate that love) but you just can't seem to connect to their same level of purpose, passion, and direction? What happens when "inspiration" is basically just a deep breath, and "service" feels like something the maid does?

I was there, not so very long ago.

You see, I had a fundamental misconception about what it means to shine in my life. I thought "shining" meant visibility, success, income, and drive. I had ample amounts of all of those things. But I still didn't feel connected, inspired, and purposeful in my life—at least, not to the degree that my peers so obviously did.

Then, I had a major epiphany: What if my current idea of "purpose" was complete and utter bullshit?

What if purpose was more than just service? What if it was simply what made me happy? In fact, what if the *whole point of life* wasn't to show up according to some grand, perfectly-stated mission, but instead to do what makes me perfectly, unapologetically happy?

It was like the roof had fallen in, and I could see the sky for the first time.

The angels weren't singing. They were slapping their foreheads, like, "Duh! Do you get it now? *Hallelujah!"*

And, finally, I did.

You see, I'd been looking at the whole thing backward. I'd been looking for purpose in service—but not in service to *me*. I'd been looking for a mission, but not at what actually lights *me* up! And, once again, I'd been looking for happiness outside of myself, instead of within.

No more. It was time for me to evolve.

When I read the stories in *SHINE!*, it was clear to me that many of these powerful women had experienced moments just like mine—moments of dramatic shift, crystal clarity, and roof removal. They had learned to shine in their lives not by living up to someone else's ideal of service, purpose, or mission, but by tuning into the only wisdom that really matters: that of their own souls.

There's a reason I hang out with these ladies. They are my friends, peers, and colleagues—but also my mirrors, my sounding boards, my teachers, and my inspiration. Now that you've read their stories, I know you will be excited to get to know them better, too.

So, if you're wondering what the next step is to start to shine in your own life, my advice is to start with what makes you glow. The things that make you happy do so for good reason. Follow where they lead, and you'll be sure to find that inner beacon you've been searching for.

And on the days when you can't muster up a full glow? Your tribe is here to lend you some glitter.

Blessings,

Bryna Haynes
Chief Editor, Inspired Living Publishing

ABOUT *Our Authors*

Tarah Abram is a designer, photo stylist, meditation teacher, advocate for mindful living, and international best-selling author. She helps busy moms and mompreneurs discover what they truly want and empowers them to get there. Tarah understands the magical connection between mind, body, and environment and how to align these elements to get women to where they are going. To learn more, visit **JuicyLivingByDesign.com.**

Transformational Life Coach and best-selling author **Felicia Baucom** believes that the path to happiness and fulfillment starts from within. She empowers women to release the stories and cultural assumptions of how their lives should be so that they can live their lives on their own terms. She inspires them to discover their truth so that they can get clear on their purpose and open up to more choices and possibilities. Connect with Felicia at **FeliciaBaucom.com.**

Crystal Cockerham, an Energy Alchemist and Transformational Mentor, guides women through the spiritual alchemical process of transformation to liberate them from the world's perceptions. The process forges and solidifies their innate connection to their inner wisdom, allows them to access their truth, empowers them to claim their sovereignty to become the woman they are meant to be, and live an authentic, connected, and joy-filled life. Learn more at **WisdomAwakens.com.**

Felicia D'Haiti is a Feng Shui and Soul Coach who guides clients in shifting perspectives and environments to move beyond perfectionism, fear, and self-imposed limitations. Felicia is an educator, as well as a Feng Shui, Space Clearing, and Soul Coaching® Teacher. She is a contributing author in *Courageous Hearts* and other best-selling books. She lives in Maryland with her husband and four children. Learn more at **FeliciaDHaiti.com.**

Susan Kay Dahl is the author of *The SEX TALK Made Easy: Keep Your Virgin From Mergin' Too SOON!* A writer, speaker, and mother of four, Susan helps busy parents make awkward conversations E.A.S.Y.—Engaging, Actionable, Simple, and Young at heart. She is the creator of Honest Answers, a program that instills confidence to talk about anything, peace of mind to sleep at night, and regret-free relationships to be proud of. Learn more at **SusanKayDahl.com**.

Maribeth Decker is an intuitive animal communicator who helps people have two-way conversations with their pets. She works with people who love their pets as much as—or more than—the people in their lives. They experience improvements in their animals' behavior and their relationship with their animals after working with Maribeth. She also helps animals' end-of-life transitions. Learn more at **SacredGrove.com**.

Monica Dubay is a spiritual life and business coach, intuitive energy healer, author, and speaker for leadership. She is on a mission to empower people who want to crush fear, shamelessly love themselves, and change the world. The Heal Your Mind Heal Your Life Transformation Program helps heart-centered women and men become leaders by finding their true purpose and embracing it. The program combines deep inner work on the mindset and belief system with powerful business coaching to bring your special gifts into a thriving business. Visit **HealYourMindHealYourLife.com** to learn more.

Jessica Dugas is an Intuitive Mentor passionate about helping women empower themselves to live with less stress and more joy. She is a multi-passionate entrepreneur bringing all her coaching skills, healing modalities, authentic intuition, and love of the moon to her Illuminate Your Spirit community and signature Your Life: Illuminated program. Outside of her business, Jessica is a wife and home-schooling mom of six beautiful children enjoying many hobbies. Learn more at **JessicaDugas.com**.

Marquetta "Martini" Goodwin began her life as a homeless child in Las Vegas, Nevada. As an adult, she survived a suicidal experience which prompted her to seek out spirituality to heal her heart and life. She's a woman who now lives life on her terms without apology and serves as a Transformational Life Coach who motivates women around the world to stop settling for less, build their self-confidence, and have the courage to take inspired action so they, too, can create the life they've always wanted. Learn more at **InternationalGirlfriend.com**.

Business Coach and Lifestyle Expert **Lisa Marie Rosati-Grantham** is the Founder of The Goddess Lifestyle Plan® and School of Magical Living™, an expert columnist for Aspire Magazine, an international best-selling author, and the leader of The Goddess Lifestyle Sisterhood™. Believing that women *can* have it all, it's Lisa's passion to teach ambitious, soul-centered women how to create an abundant life and prosperous laptop business they love! Lisa exemplifies the Goddess Lifestyle as she embraces her powerful feminine nature with pride and encourages other women to do the same. Learn more at **GoddessLifestylePlan.com.**

Michele Greer is a transformational and lifestyle coach who helps women rewrite their stories of pain, lack, and struggle that keep them from living their best lives. Michele birthed her "Beyond Brave" mission after her own life-altering experience. Using the same mindset strategies and self-love rituals she used to transform her own life, she empowers and supports women who are caught up in the story of their past, helps them rewrite their story, and create a life of happiness, joy, and fulfillment. Learn more at **MicheleGreer.com.**

Kelley Grimes, MSW, is a counselor, speaker, international best-selling author, expert columnist for Aspire Magazine, and self-nurturing expert. She is passionate about empowering overwhelmed and exhausted individuals to live with more peace, joy, and meaning through the practice of self-nurturing. Kelley also provides professional and leadership development to organizations dedicated to making the world a better place. She is married to an artist, has two empowered daughters, and loves singing with a small women's group. Learn more at **CultivatingPeaceandJoy.com.**

Kris Groth is a spiritual mentor, energy healer, and international best-selling author. She is passionate about helping people connect more deeply to their truth to live a soul-inspired life. She uses her gifts and wisdom to heal your heart, nurture your soul, and illuminate your path. She offers healing and mentoring sessions by phone, and sound healing meditations with crystal singing bowls. Her best-selling novel, *Soul-iloquy: A Novel of Healing, Soul Connection & Passion,* is now available at **KrisGroth.com.**

Kathleen Gubitosi, MA is an award-winning businesswoman, performing artist, metaphysical practitioner, and Creatrix of *The Magic of Voice Alchemy™,* a holistic approach to voice health and personal/professional image enhancement. She guides emerging heart-centered feminine leaders to set their sacred message free and connect deeply with their ideal audiences at home, at work, and on stage, by channeling the most potent gift on earth: their voices. Learn more at **KathleenGubitosi.com.**

Dr. Catherine Hayes, CPCC is a dual-certified Professional Co-Active Coach; a Certified Riso-Hudson Enneagram Teacher and International Enneagram Association (IEA) Certified Professional and Accredited Teacher; an international best-selling author; a member of the Forbes Coaches Council; a speaker; and a highly-regarded influencer in the leadership field. She holds a DMD from Tufts University and Masters and Doctoral degrees in Epidemiology from Harvard University. She coaches leaders to uncover the truth of who they are so they can live and lead from their highest potential. Learn more at **CatherineHayesCoaching.com.**

Jami Hearn, a transformational intuitive prosperity coach, specializes in working with spiritual women to achieve their divine abundance. She is an expert contributor to *Aspire Magazine*, holds certifications as an Akashic Records Practitioner, and is an Evidential Medium. Having gone from an unfulfilling career as an attorney to a thriving international coaching practice, Jami's passion is supporting and encouraging women to live their soul's purpose with ease and grace, while fulfilling their truest desires. Learn more at **JamiHearn.com.**

Cindy Hively is an internationally-acclaimed Intuitive Healing Coach, Priestess, Goddess Creatrix of In Her Fullness, and a #1 best-selling author. Her clients lovingly call her "transformational," as she uncovers the root cause to healing their emotional pain and illness. She helps women retrain their conscious and subconscious minds to release unhelpful habits and beliefs, allowing them to pursue their hopes and dreams by living a spiritual and healthy lifestyle. Learn more at **InHerFullness.com.**

Deborah Kevin loves helping visionary entrepreneurs attract their ideal clients by tapping into and sharing their stories of healing and truth. She's a member of the Association of Writing Professionals, Association of Ghostwriters, and the National Association of Memoir Writers. Ms. Kevin is an associate editor with Inspired Living Publishing and a former online editor of *Little Patuxent Review.* Her passions include travel, cooking, hiking, and kayaking. She lives with her family in Maryland. Visit **DeborahKevin.com** to learn more.

Marcia Mariner, a sacred wealth coach and global leader of the new wealth consciousness, coaches mission-driven women who are ready to unleash their power, discover their authentic selves, and build their dream lives. Marcia radically embodies her teachings by continually committing herself to her growth. She is the founder of Wealthy Woman Within Sacred Wealth Community and Sacred Wealth Immersion Program. Learn more about Marcia and her work at **MarciaMariner.com.**

Nicole Meltzer is the founder and director of BalancedUAcademy.com, an online academy for personal development and empowerment. She lives with her husband, Elliott, and their two sons, Liam and Ethan, north of Toronto in Newmarket, Ontario. Learn more at **BalancedUAcademy.com.**

Kelly Mishell, a certified Law of Attraction Life Coach and inspirational speaker, is dedicated to guiding you away from what's wrong in your life and toward the amazing life you are meant to have. It is her mission to help women at any age find their inner spark of greatness and deliberately create successful, balanced, joyful lives they love. Learn more at **KellyMishell.com.**

Whether in her books, sacred retreats, authentic leadership trainings or 1:1 coaching, **Lizete Morais** empowers passionate, professional women around the world to expand their lives, careers, and relationships. Using the powerful principles of awakening, awareness, and authenticity, she supports her clients to identify and overcome the core issues standing between them and their true desires. Lizete has discovered that the journey of development and living your authentic voice, isn't about being this other version of yourself—it's about discovering the voice that you truly are and healing and unravelling everything that took you out of alignment with your intuitive knowing and the perfection you already are. Learn more at **AuthenticVoice.co**.

Consciously merging her practical tools as a psychologist with her intuitive and spiritual gifts, Intuitive Psychologist **Dr. Debra L. Reble** empowers women to connect with their hearts, release fear and anxiety, and supports them in breaking through their energetic and spiritual blocks to self-love so they can live authentically. Debra is the international best-selling author of *Being Love: How Loving Yourself Creates Ripples of Transformation in Your Relationships and the World* (Inspired Living Publishing) as well as a contributing author to many best-selling books. Debra is a sought-after speaker and media guest and is the host of the popular Soul-Hearted Living Podcast on iTunes and the creator of the program, "Anxiety RX: Balm for the Soul." Learn more at **DebraReble.com**.

Ann Sanfelippo is a #1 international best-selling author, speaker, coach, and founder of The Wealth Attraction Academy, a company dedicated to providing women with the tools and resources they need to manifest an abundant life of their dreams—financially, emotionally, and spiritually. She has studied the philosophies of the most powerful influencers in the world, both past and present; these incredible mentors helped propelled her to outstanding success. Now, she shares her formula with the world. Learn more at **WealthAttractionAcademy.com.**

ABOUT
Our Publisher

Linda Joy & Inspired Living Publishing

Founded in 2010 by Inspirational Catalyst, radio show host, and *Aspire Magazine* Publisher Linda Joy, Inspired Living Publishing (ILP) is an international best-selling inspirational boutique publishing company dedicated to spreading a message of love, positivity, feminine wisdom, and self-empowerment to women of all ages, backgrounds, and life paths. Linda's multimedia brands reach over 44,000 subscribers and a social media community of over 24,000 women.

Through our highly-successful anthology division, we have brought eight books and over 300 visionary female authors to best-seller status. Our powerful, high-visibility publishing, marketing, and list-building packages have brought these authors—all visionary entrepreneurs, coaches, therapists, and health practitioners—the positive, dynamic exposure they need to attract their ideal audience and thrive in their businesses.

Inspired Living Publishing also publishes single-author books by visionary female authors whose messages are aligned with Linda's philosophy of authenticity, empowerment, and personal transformation.

Recent best-selling releases include *Everything Is Going to Be Okay: From the Projects to Harvard to Freedom* by Dr. Catherine Hayes, CPCC; *Awakening to Life: Your Sacred Guide to Consciously Creating a Life of Purpose, Magic, and Miracles* by Patricia Young; the award-winning *Being Love: How Loving Yourself Creates Ripples of Transformation in Your Relationships and the World*, by Dr. Debra L. Reble; and the multiple award-winning *The Art of Inspiration: An Editor's Guide to Writing Powerful, Effective Inspirational & Personal Development Books*, by ILP Chief Editor Bryna Haynes.

ILP's family of authors reap the benefits of being a part of a sacred family of inspirational multimedia brands which deliver the best in transformational and empowering content across a wide range of platforms. Our hybrid publishing packages and *à la carte* marketing and media packages provide visionary female authors with access to our proven best-seller model and high-profile multimedia exposure across all of Linda's imprints (including *Aspire Magazine*, the "Inspired Conversations" radio show on OMTimes Radio, the Inspired Living Giveaway, Inspired Living Secrets, and exposure to Linda's loyal personal audience of over 44,000 women).

If you're ready to publish your transformational book, or share your story in one of ours, we invite you to join us! Learn more about our publishing services at **InspiredLivingPublishing.com**.

Inspired Living Publishing ~ Transforming Women's Lives, One Story at a Time™

If you enjoyed this book, visit
InspiredLivingPublishing.com
and sign up for ILP's e-zine to receive news about hot new releases, promotions, and information on exciting author events.

ABOUT *Our Editor*

Bryna Haynes

Word alchemist Bryna Haynes is the founder of The Heart of Writing, the chief editor for Inspired Living Publishing, and the best-selling author of the multiple-award-winning book, *The Art of Inspiration: An Editor's Guide to Writing Powerful, Effective Inspirational & Personal Development Books* (2016). Her heart-centered book development coaching, editing services, and online courses are designed to help inspired writers move through their blocks and perceived limitations, connect with their authentic voices, and create world-changing written works that transform their lives and businesses.

Bryna's editing portfolio includes numerous successful non-fiction titles, including all of Inspired Living Publishing's best-selling print anthologies.

Through her company, The Heart of Writing, Bryna and her team offer educational tools, online writing courses, creative support and coaching, and professional editing services for authors, business owners, and bloggers in all genres.

Bryna is also the founder of Choose Your Evolution™, a service project she jokingly calls, "The Law of Attraction for Skeptics." CYE is dedicated to empowering people as true creators in their lives through inspiration, motivation, and the art of experiential creation.

Bryna lives in Rhode Island with her husband, Matthew, and their daughters, Áine and Aelyn. When she's not writing, you can find her reading epic fantasy, doing "mama stuff," and expounding on metaphysics, quantum science, and spiritual philosophy to anyone who will listen.

Learn more about Bryna's work at **TheHeartofWriting.com** and **ChooseYourEvolution.blog.**